CLEMSON

DAILY DEVOTIONS FOR DIE-HARD FANS

TIGERS

CLEMSON

Daily Devotions for Die-Hard Fans: Clemson Tigers
© 2009 Ed McMinn

Library of Congress Cataloging-in-Publication Data
13 ISBN Digit ISBN: 978-0-9801749-6-0

Manufactured in the United States of America.

For bulk purchases or to request the author for speaking engagements, email contact@extrapointpublishers.com.

Go to http://www.die-hardfans.com for information about other titles in the series.

Cover and interior design by Slynn McMinn.

TIGERS

*Dedicated
to the greater glory
of God.*

DAY 1

IN THE BEGINNING

Read Genesis 1, 2:1-3.

"God saw all that he had made, and it was very good" (v. 1:31).

This country is in wretched condition, no money and nothing to sell. Everyone is ruined, and those that can are leaving." Out of that woeful assessment arose Clemson University.

Thomas Green Clemson spoke those words after the Civil War. He had come to South Carolina in 1838 when he married the daughter of John C. Calhoun. When he died in 1888, he bequeathed his plantation and a considerable sum to establish a new state school for agricultural and military education. In November 1889, Clemson Agricultural College was established.

The new college opened its doors in July 1893 as an all-male, all-military school with an initial enrollment of 446 cadets. Not until 1955 did the college change to "civilian" status and admit coeds. In 1964 the college was renamed Clemson University.

In 1895, Walter Merritt Riggs came to the new college as professor of engineering. He brought with him a love for this new game called football he had played as an undergraduate at Auburn. On Sept. 30, 1896, a group of thirty students met in the barracks and organized a football aid association. They asked Professor Riggs to coach the school's first football team.

Twenty-one students began practice on Oct. 5. On Oct. 28, Clemson played its first intercollegiate football game, defeating

TIGERS

Furman 14-6 in Greenville. Charlie Gentry scored Clemson's first touchdown.

The cadets completed their first season with a 2-1 record by defeating Wofford 16-0 on Nov. 21. When the team arrived on campus, the cadets and the faculty members "led the team around in a buggy led by a torchlight procession and proceeded to go all over campus."

Football fever had formally begun at Clemson College.

Beginnings are important, but what we make of them is even more important. Consider, for example, how far the Clemson football program has come since that first season. Every morning, you get a gift from God: a new beginning. God hands to you as an expression of divine love a new day full of promise and the chance to right the wrongs in your life. You can use the day to pay a debt, start a new relationship, replace a burned-out light bulb, tell your family you love them, chase a dream, solve a nagging problem . . . or not.

God simply provides the gift. How you use it is up to you. People often talk wistfully about starting over or making a new beginning. God gives you the chance with the dawning of every new day. You have the chance today to make things right – and that includes your relationship with God.

The most important key to achieving great success is to decide upon your goal and launch, get started, take action, move.
-- John Wooden

Every day is not just a dawn;
it is a precious chance to start over or begin anew.

DAY 2

A LONG SHOT

Read Matthew 9:9-13.

"[Jesus] saw a man named Matthew sitting at the tax collector's booth. 'Follow me,' he told him, and Matthew got up and followed him" (v. 9).

The Clemson Tigers were unranked entering the 1981 football season, a long shot for the national championship. After the first quarter of the first game, they were an even longer shot.

The Tigers were scheduled to open the season against Villanova until the school announced in March it was giving up football. Attempts to line up a game with other of Villanova's opponents failed, and so the Wofford Terriers, an NAIA school, were a last-minute replacement. All they did was come into Memorial Stadium on Sept. 5, take the opening kickoff, and march to the Clemson seven before kicking a field goal. Donald Igwebuike's 52-yard field goal tied the game, and the first quarter ended with that 3-3 score.

Surely nobody associated with Clemson football was thinking national championship at that moment. Perhaps many were hoping the Tigers would simply not get embarrassed by the upstarts from Spartanburg.

They didn't. Quarterback Homer Jordan threw for two touchdowns and ran for two more in rolling up 235 yards of total offense. Defensive back Terry Kinard started his march toward an All-American season with eleven tackles. The Tigers led 17-3 at halftime and 31-3 after three quarters on their way to a 45-10 win.

Some aspects of the game, though, left the Tigers with a lot to work on. Wofford managed 165 yards rushing, the most of any team that season except Nebraska. The Terriers also had the ball for 35 minutes, the only team all year to have a time-of-possession advantage over the Tigers.

The win failed to garner Clemson a single vote in the top 20. The Tigers were still long shots.

Matthew the tax collector was another long shot, an unlikely person to be a confidant of the Son of God. While we may not get all warm and fuzzy about the IRS, our government's revenue agents are nothing like Matthew and his ilk. He bought a franchise, paying the Roman Empire for the privilege of bullying and stealing everything he could from his own people. Tax collectors of the time were "despicable, vile, unprincipled scoundrels."

And yet, Jesus said only two words to this lowlife: "Follow me." Jesus knew that this long shot would make an excellent disciple.

It's the same with us. While we may not be quite as vile as Matthew was, none of us can stand before God with our hands clean and our hearts pure. We are all impossibly long shots to enter God's Heaven. That is, until we do what Matthew did: get up and follow Jesus.

Overcoming challenges should never be considered a long shot.
-- Mother of disabled child on MightyMikeBasketball.com

Only through Jesus does our status change from being long shots to enter God's Kingdom to being heavy favorites.

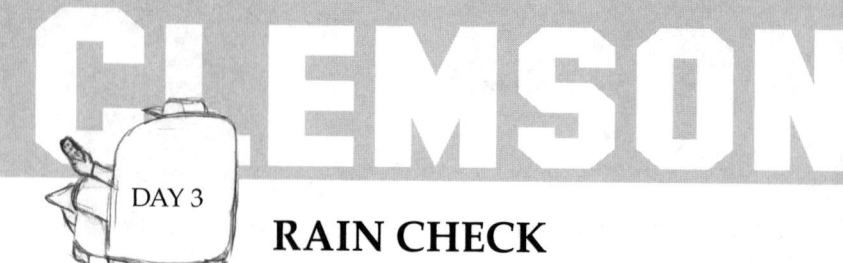

RAIN CHECK

Read Genesis 9:8-17.

*"I establish my covenant with you: Never again will all
life be cut off by the waters of a flood; never again will
there be a flood to destroy the earth" (v. 11).*

It was called the "prettiest thunderstorm ever." For Clemson
baseball fans, it was.

In 1958, legendary coach Bill Wilhelm's first season, Clemson
finished the ACC season tied with North Carolina. Only one
team from each conference was selected for the district playoffs,
so a one-game playoff was required. The Tigers won 4-1 with Bud
Spiers getting an RBI single to lead a three-run outburst in the
top of the first.

At the regionals in Gastonia, Clemson lost the first-round game
to SEC champion Florida. After that, it was win-or-go-home for
the Tigers. So they took the field and promptly fell behind George
Washington 7-0 by the bottom of the second inning. Then came
that "prettiest thunderstorm ever," washing everything out, since
the rules then required the game to go five innings or be restarted
from scratch.

Given a second chance by the rain, the Tigers whipped GW
4-2 behind sophomore righthander Ed Lakey. Clemson then blew
a 5-0 lead against FSU, but won 10-7 in ten innings on a bases-
loaded double from Spiers.

The rain wasn't around to bail them out when the Tigers fell behind Florida 10-5 to start the sixth. This time, though, Clemson didn't need a break from the weather, rallying for a 15-14 win with a single run in the bottom of the ninth. Harold Stowe then pitched the game of his career, striking out 17, as the Tigers managed only two hits but scored three runs to whip Florida again 3-1.

After that "prettiest thunderstorm ever," the Tigers won four straight to advance to the College World Series.

The kids are on go for their picnic. Your golf game is set. You have ribeyes and smoked sausage ready for the grill when the gang comes over tonight. And then it rains.

Sometimes you can slog on through a downpour. Often, however, as it did with George Washington and Clemson, the rain simply washes away your carefully laid plans, and you can't do anything about it.

Rain falls when and where it wants to without checking with you. It answers only to God, the one who controls the heavens from which it comes, the ground on which it falls, and everything in between -- territory that should include you. Though God has absolute dominance over the rain, he will take control of your life only if you let him. In daily seeking his will for your life, you discover that you can live so as to be walking in the sunshine even when it's raining.

Don't pray when it rains if you don't pray when the sun shines.
-- Pitcher and philosopher Leroy "Satchel" Paige

Into each life some rain must fall,
but you can live in the glorious light of God's love
even during a downpour.

UNTIL IT HURTS

Read Isaiah 53.

"He was despised and rejected by men, a man of sorrows, and familiar with suffering" (v. 3a).

He was hit so hard he could barely make it to the sideline, out for the rest of the game for sure. Until C.J. Spiller showed everyone that pain wasn't going to stop him.

Combining with backfield mate James Davis to form the Clemson duo "Thunder and Lightning," Spiller virtually carried the Tigers to a win over Boston College on Nov. 1, 2008. That was after he needed to be carried from the field himself.

Clemson led 17-0 in the third quarter when Spiller appeared to sew up the win with a 40-yard reception on a screen pass. The play, however, was a disaster on two levels. First, a holding penalty negated the gain. Second, Spiller was injured on the play. "I thought it was his hamstring, because that's what's been hurt, but it ended up he just got knocked a little cuckoo," said Coach Dabo Swinney.

Perhaps engaging in wishful thinking, the Boston College PA announcer declared Spiller was out of the game. "He shook it off," Swinney declared. Did he ever. Spiller returned to set a school record and set up the winning touchdown in the 27-21 Tiger win, Swinney's first as the interim head coach. "Twenty-eight (Spiller's number) was the difference down the stretch for sure," Swinney said.

When Spiller returned, he had two receptions early in the fourth quarter that gave him 105 yards for the game, a new Clemson record for a running back. Meanwhile, the 17-0 lead turned into a 21-17 deficit. After BC grabbed the lead, Spiller returned the ensuing kickoff 64 yards to set up Aaron Kelly's game-winning touchdown reception with 7:10 left.

Even if he had been in pain, Spiller said, "I would've told [the trainers] I was ready to go."

Unlike C.J. Spiller, we don't usually include actual physical pain and suffering as part of the price we are willing to pay to succeed. We'll work overtime, we may neglect our family, we may even work ourselves into exhaustion, but actual pain, suffering, and agony? They are definitely not part of our job description. What would we give up to avoid pain and suffering whether on the job or in our daily lives? Everything?

Merely by choosing to, Jesus could have easily evaded the horrific pain and suffering he underwent. Instead, he opted for his love for you over his own well-being, and agony was part of his decision for love.

Now we all face the question: How far do we go with Jesus? Do we bail out on him when it gets inconvenient? Or do we walk with him all the way even when it hurts – just as Jesus did for us?

Sometimes you have to play with a little pain.

– C.J. Spiller

We must decide whether we'll walk all the way with Jesus, even when it hurts, or whether we'll bail out when faith gets inconvenient.

DAY 5

THE NIGHTMARE

Read Mark 1:21-27.

"Have you come to destroy us? I know who you are – the Holy one of God!" (v. 24)

Clemson tennis star Mimi Burgos knew exactly what her worst nightmare would be: playing herself.

Burgos was a key member of the Tiger women's teams from 1989-92. A four-year letterman, she won 137 singles and doubles matches. She played #1 singles for two years and #1 doubles all four years. She was the MVP of the 25th-ranked 1991 team and was All-ACC in 1990, '91, and '92.

Burgos didn't stand on the baseline and blast forehands past her bedazzled opponents. She was, rather, one of Clemson's more interesting players. "I'm really different," she admitted. What she did was attempt to confuse and flummox her opponents with what she called "weird stuff."

Analyzing herself, Burgos said that if you watched her play, "You wouldn't think I'm that good of a player because it seems like I probably miss-hit every single ball." That's because she was doing the "weird stuff" to it.

Burgos did anything she could to gain an advantage. "I can do a lot with a ball," she said. "I can slice, I can top spin, I can drop shot, I can serve and volley. . . . I try to do a lot of different things. I try to have fun with it. . . . I get really bored easily."

In other words, she was every player's nightmare – even her

own. "I couldn't even imagine playing myself," she once said. "It would be a nightmare."

Her affinity for "weird stuff" perhaps disguised an extremely good and intense player. After a disappointing sophomore season, the San Diego native went to San Francisco during the summer and trained with her brother, a professional teacher and her coach growing up.

Which only made the nightmare worse for her opponents.

Falling. Drowning. Standing naked in a crowded room. They're nightmares, dreams that jolt us from our sleep in anxiety or downright terror. The film industry has used our common nightmares to create horror movies that allow us to experience our fears vicariously. This includes the formulaic "evil vs. good" movies in which demons and the like render good virtually helpless in the face of their power and ruthlessness.

The spiritual truth, though, is that it is evil that has come face to face with its worst nightmare: Jesus. We seem to understand that our basic mission as Jesus' followers is to further his kingdom and change the world through emulating him in the way we live and love others. But do we appreciate that in truly living for Jesus, we are daily tormenting the very devil himself?

Satan and his lackeys quake in fear before the power of almighty God that is in us through Jesus.

I can't have a nightmare tonight. I've just lived through one.
-- Darrell Imhoff, the opposing center the night Wilt Chamberlain
scored 100 points

As the followers of Jesus Christ, we are the stuff of Satan's nightmares.

YOU NEVER KNOW

Read Exodus 3:1-12.

"But Moses said to God, 'Who am I, that I should go to Pharaoh and bring the Israelites out of Egypt?' And God said, 'I will be with you" (vv. 11-12a).

Danny Ford once used an astoundingly unique way of illustrating to his players that they never know what they can do.

Ken Tysiac tells the story that one day before a big game that weekend, Ford had some rather unusual looking fried meat brought to his players. Ford had a well deserved reputation among his players as a prankster. For instance, when offensive line coach Larry Van Der Heyden received a summons for jury duty, Ford directed him to promotions director Allison Dalton to get him excused. Heyden forget all about it until two policemen showed up at the practice field and told the coach he was under arrest for missing jury duty. Van Der Heyden naturally panicked and sputtered his protestation that it was all a mistake. The officers handcuffed him and placed him in their car. Only then did a laughing Ford, who had conveniently ignored the whole affair until then, saunter over to the car and reveal it was all a gag.

So, not surprisingly, the players were suspicious about that strange meat their coach was offering them. While some declined, many sampled it. "They were pretty good, actually," said fullback Jeff McCall. The players agreed with McCall's appraisal and that the meat tasted like chicken. Only then did Ford disclose that they had just dined on mountain oysters: cows' testicles.

As Tysiak put it, the coach's revelation "of course, brought about bedlam." "There were people falling on the floor, running out of the room, spitting," said wide receiver Jerry Gaillard. "It was pretty hilarious."

Ford then delivered his point to his players: You never know what you can do so don't put limitations on yourselves.

Coach Danny Ford's message rings true in all areas of life. You never know what you can do until you want to bad enough or until you have to. Serving in the military, maybe even in combat. Standing by a friend while everyone else unjustly excoriates her. Undergoing agonizing medical treatment and managing to smile. You never know what life will demand of you.

It's that way too in your relationship with God. As Moses discovered, you never know where or when God will call you or what God will ask of you. You do know that God expects you to be faithful and willing to trust him even when he calls you to tasks that daunt and dismay you.

You can respond faithfully to whatever God calls you to do for him. That's because even though you never know what lies ahead, you do know that God will both lead you and provide what you need.

There's one word to describe baseball: You never know.
— Yogi Berra

You never know what God will ask you to do,
but you always know he will provide
everything you need to do it.

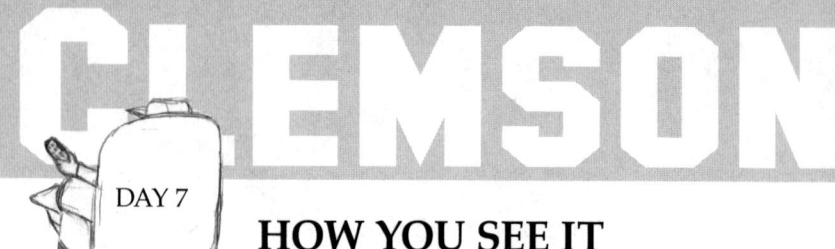

HOW YOU SEE IT

Read John 20:11-18.

"Mary stood outside the tomb crying" (v. 11).

Their hopes for a fourth straight trip to the NCAA dashed, the Tigers rediscovered the fun of playing college basketball in an unexpected place.

On March 4, 1999, the Tiger men lost in overtime to FSU in the opening round of the ACC Tournament. At the postgame press conference, a reporter asked senior guard Terrell McIntyre, the ACC's leading scorer, if he would be interested in playing in the NIT, the consolation prize for teams that don't make it into the Big Dance. Coach Larry Shyatt thought McIntyre's response was "remarkable. . . . He never batted an eyelash." "As a player you never want to have your season end," McIntyre said.

So after seasons of 18-11, 23-10, and 18-14 that included two wins in the NCAA Tournament and a big win over defending national champion Kentucky, the Tigers were bound for the lesser tournament. Surely in their disappointment, they would go through the motions, get it over with, and exit the tournament as soon as possible.

Not at all. Instead, in the NIT the Tigers learned "how to smile again. How to laugh. And how to sing in the locker room." They also played some good basketball again. "We're playing for fun, playing to have a good time and try[ing] to make the most of what we've got," senior center Tom Wideman said.

The Tigers could well have regarded the NIT as a tournament for losers, but instead they had a blast, whipping Georgia, Rutgers, Butler, and Xavier before losing a thriller in the finals to California 61-60. They wound up on a definite high note with 20 wins for the season.

Your perspective goes a long way toward determining whether you slink through life amid despair, anger, and hopelessness or stride boldly through life with joy and hope. Whether you have fun and win games or hang your head and wish you weren't playing.

Mary is a good example. On that first Easter morning, she stood by Jesus' tomb crying, her heart broken, because she still viewed everything through the perspective of Jesus' death. But how her attitude, her heart, and her life changed when she saw the morning through the perspective of Jesus' resurrection.

So it is with life and death for all of us. You can't avoid death, but you can determine how you perceive it. Is it fearful, dark, fraught with peril and uncertainty? Or is it a simple little passageway to glory, the light, and loved ones, an elevator ride to paradise?

It's a matter of perspective that depends totally on whether or not you're standing by Jesus' side when it arrives.

For some people it's the end of the rainbow, but for us it's the end of the finish line.
— *Rower Larisa Healy*

Whether death is your worst enemy or a solicitous chauffeur is a matter of perspective.

DAY 8

SUPERSTITION

Read 1 Samuel 28:3-20.

"Saul then said to his attendants, 'Find me a woman who is a medium, so I may go and inquire of her'" (v. 7).

The "mystical powers" of Howard's Rock. That's the only way Frank Howard could account for Clemson's win over Virginia in 1966.

During Frank Howard's long tenure as head football coach, Memorial Stadium became more familiarly known as Death Valley. In the early 1950s, a Clemson graduate presented Howard a rock he had retrieved while on a vacation through Death Valley, Calif. He figured Clemson's Death Valley should have a rock from the real Death Valley. After the rock lay around his office for several years, Howard told IPTAY Executive Secretary Gene Willimon to do something with it. What Willimon did was inspired genius. He had the rock mounted on a pedestal on the top of the hill at the east end of the stadium where the Tigers make their famous entrance.

The football players did not begin the ritual of touching the rock as they ran down the hill until 1967, but the legend of the rock's powers began with the 40-35 win over Virginia in 1966. Clemson won despite losing five fumbles and giving up 429 yards of offense. "It was obvious some kind of strange powers must have been with the Tigers on this particular day."

The superstitious Howard once told his players that if they gave all they had he would let them "rub my rock, and it'll give you supernatural powers." The story got out, and a woman wrote to Howard to say it was no wonder he didn't win more games since he believed in rocks instead of God. "She said if I'd've believed in God instead of rocks, I would've been a lot better coach."

Black cats are right pretty. A medium is s steak. A key chain with a rabbit's foot wasn't too lucky for the rabbit. And what in the world is a blarney stone? About as superstitious as you get is to say "God bless you" when somebody sneezes or to rub Howard's Rock before a game.

You look indulgently upon good-luck charms, tarot cards, astrology, palm readers, and the like; they're really just amusing and harmless. So what's the problem? Nothing as long as you conduct yourself with the belief that superstitious objects and rituals – from broken mirrors to your daily horoscope –can't bring about good or bad luck. You aren't willing to let such notions and nonsense rule your life.

The danger of superstition lies in its ability to lure you into trusting it, thus allowing it some degree of influence over your life. In that case, it subverts God's rightful place.

Whether or not it's superstition, something does rule your life. It should be God – and God alone.

I don't believe in a jinx or a hex. Winning depends on how well you block and tackle.

-- *Shug Jordan*

Superstitions may not rule your life, but something does; it should be God and God alone.

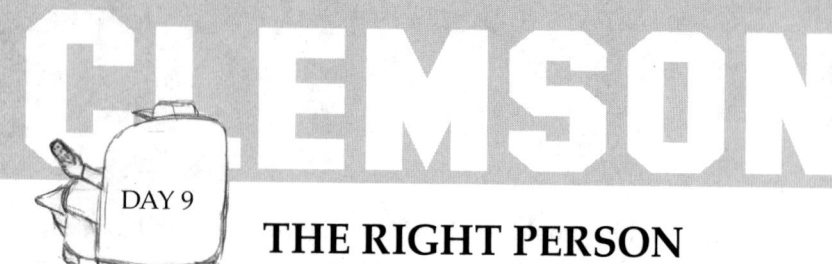

THE RIGHT PERSON

Read Matthew 26:47-50; 27:1-10.

"The betrayer had arranged a signal with them: 'The one I kiss is the man; arrest him.' Going at once to Jesus, Judas said, 'Greetings, Rabbi!' and kissed him" (vv. 48-49).

Clemson football coach Jess Neely found the right man for a job he needed done, one who followed his instructions exactly – even when that meant Neely couldn't join his team on the field for a game.

Neely took over the Tiger program in 1931 and coached for nine seasons. He had a wire fence installed around Riggs Field for crowd control and secured a state patrolman to guard the playing field on game days. Neely gave him explicit instructions: "Your job is to see that nobody – nobody – gets through this gate without a sideline ticket."

An hour later, the Tigers charged out of their dressing room for a game, the players and assistant coaches dutifully flashing their sideline passes. Neely walked decorously behind his team until the state patrolman stopped him and asked for his ticket. A surprised Neely reminded the trooper who he was. "I don't know you or nobody," the patrolman barked. "I was told not to let nobody in without a ticket and nobody's gonna get in without one." "I'm who told you," an exasperated Neely said, "and I got to get in there with my team."

"Ain't nobody getting in here without a ticket. And no loitering around the gate," the trooper declared, ending the discussion.

A remarkably restrained Neely walked down the wire fence, secured a pass from an assistant coach, and passed by the still unsmiling trooper. The coach later wrote a letter to the state highway department requesting that the trooper be assigned to that same gate at all future Clemson games.

Jess Neely had found the right man for the job.

What do you want to be when you grow up? Somehow you are supposed to know the answer to that question when you're a teenager, the time in life when common sense and logic are at their lowest ebb.

Long after those halcyon teen years are left behind, you may still be trying to figure out what you'll be when you grow up, and so you make frequent career changes. You chase the job that gives you not just financial rewards but also some personal satisfaction and sense of accomplishment. You desire a profession that uses your abilities, that you enjoy doing, and that gives you a sense of contributing to something bigger than yourself.

God, too, wants you in the right job, one that he has designed specifically for you. After all, even Judas was the right man for what God needed done. To do his work, God gave you abilities, talents, and passions. Do what you do best and what you love -- just do it for God.

The price of success is hard work and dedication to the job at hand.
-- Vince Lombardi

God has a job for you, one for which he gave you particular talents, abilities, and passions.

TEACHER'S PET

Read John 3:1-16.

"[Nicodemus] came to Jesus at night and said, 'Rabbi, we know you are a teacher who has come from God'" (v. 2).

Clemson's most successful basketball coach ever was initially the third choice for the job and considered himself a teacher as much as a coach.

In his eighteen years as head coach of the Lady Tiger basketball team, Jim Davis won 355 games, making him the winningest basketball coach in school history. He led Clemson to 14 NCAA Tournament appearances and 11 final national rankings. His team won at least twenty games eleven times, and fifty-one times his Tigers beat nationally ranked teams.

Davis came to Clemson in 1987 when Annie Tribble retired after eleven years. Senior associate athletics director Dwight Rainey interviewed twelve people for the job; Davis was the twelfth and was a long shot at best since Rainey was on record as saying he preferred to hire a woman. He offered the job to two other candidates, who turned him down. He then turned to Davis, whose impact on the program was immediate. He turned a team that was 7-21 the year before into a 21-9 powerhouse that advanced to the second round of the NCAA Tournament.

For all his coaching success, Davis always considered what he did as a form of teaching. One writer said Davis "approaches his job like a math teacher preparing for a calculus class. His course is Basketball 301." The finals are the ACC Tournament. Davis basically agreed with that analysis. "I've always approached coaching like it was a classroom situation," Davis once said. "Just like that biology teacher, or an English teacher, or whatever. They have a subject matter to teach, and I have a subject matter to teach."

And judging from the results, he taught his subject matter quite well.

You can read this book, break 90 on the golf course, and succeed at your job because somebody taught you. And as you learn, you become the teacher yourself. You teach your children how to play Monopoly and how to drive a car. You show rookies the ropes at the office and teach baseball's basics to Little Leaguers.

This pattern of learning and then teaching includes your spiritual life also. Somebody taught you about Jesus, and this, too, you must pass on. Jesus came to teach a truth the religious teachers and the powerful of his day did not want to hear. Little has changed in that regard, as the world today often reacts with scorn and disdain to Jesus' message.

Nothing, not even death itself, could stop Jesus from teaching his lesson of life and salvation. So should nothing stop you from teaching life's most important lesson: Jesus saves.

The only reason we make good role models is because you guys look up to athletes. . . . The real role models should be your parents and teachers!

-- NFL player Dante Hall

**In life, you lean and then you teach,
which includes learning and teaching about Jesus,
the most important lesson of all.**

HANGING IN THERE

Read Mark 14:32-42.

"'Father,' he said, 'everything is possible for you. Take this cup from me. Yet not what I will, but what you will'" (v. 36).

Fitzhugh Lee Bethea learned about persistence as a football walk-on at Clemson. It later helped him get his life back after an awful car wreck.

Bethea was recruited by only a few small schools after high school, so he walked on at Clemson in 1980. The first day the walk-ons met, Coach Danny Ford asked them to stand up, tell something about themselves, and say what position they played. To his dismay, Bethea learned the room was full of undersized defensive backs, the position he played the most in high school. So when his time came, he said he played wide receiver "because no one else had said they were a receiver. I thought I would have a better chance to play."

He was on the scout team and hung in there through a brutal freshman season of continually getting nailed at practice. His persistence paid off when he got to dress out for all the home games and go to the road games his sophomore season. He got some playing time his junior season and despite an influx of talented true receivers, he played enough his senior season, 1983, to letter. About 70 walk-ons had been at that first meeting, but only "five or ten of us stayed the entire four years."

TIGERS

Bethea's persistence was challenged again in 1997 when he was severely injured in a vehicle accident. He was in a back brace and bedridden for six months; his doctors were unsure of his long-term prognosis. Bethea said, "Once again I had to rely on persistence. . . . Just like when I was told I would never play college football. I *did* play and I *did* fully recover."

Life is tough; it inevitably beats us up and kicks us around some. But life has four quarters, and so here we are, still standing, still in the game. Like Fitzhugh Lee Bethea and his dogged persistence that carried him through some challenging times, we know that we can never win if we don't finish. We emerge as winners and champions only if we never give up, if we just see it through.

Interestingly, Jesus has been in the same situation. On that awful night in the garden, Jesus understood the nature of the suffering he was about to undergo, and he begged God to take it from him. In the end, though, he yielded to God's will and surrendered his own.

Even in the matter of persistence, Jesus is our example. As he did, we push doggedly and determinedly ahead – following God's will for our lives -- no matter how hard it gets. And we can do it because God is with us.

If you put forth the effort, God will be there to help.
– Fitzhugh Lee Bethea

**It's tough to keep going no matter what,
but you have the power of almighty God
to pull you through.**

DAY 12

ONE TOUGH COOKIE

Read 2 Corinthians 11:21b-29.

"Besides everything else, I face daily the pressure of my concern for all the churches" (v. 28).

This won't take long. That little guy from Clemson is as tough as nails."

The speaker was a collegiate golf coach; the occasion was the beginning of a playoff to decide the 1997 NCAA men's golf champion; the player he was speaking about was Clemson junior Charles Warren.

As it turned out, the coach knew exactly what he was talking about.

Warren fired a brilliant 67 in the final round and came from six shots behind on the final day to edge two golfers by one stroke and force a playoff with Brad Elder of Texas.

Warren came into the tournament as the ACC champion and a two-time All-America, but he wasn't necessarily a favorite to win. The ACC Tournament had been his first championship of what until then was a difficult season.

But he charged from the pack the last day with a surge on the back nine. His coach, Larry Penley, saw it coming. "Charles is a tough, tough nut," he said. "I could tell today on the back side, when I started walking with him on No. 13, that he was just incredibly focused. . . . Once I saw him in that frame of mind, I knew it was just a matter of time before he made some birdies."

But the "tough, tough nut" still had a sudden-death playoff to win. Just as that prescient coach had said, however, it didn't take long. Warren nailed a putt for par on the first hole to become the first NCAA solo event champion in Clemson history.

The tough nut didn't crack.

You don't have to be a legendary Clemson golfer to be tough. In America today, toughness isn't restricted to physical accomplishments and brute strength. Going to work every morning even when you feel bad, sticking by your rules for your children in a society that ridicules parental authority, making hard decisions about your aging parents' care often over their objections — you've got to be tough every day just to live honorably, decently, and justly.

Living faithfully requires toughness too, though in America chances are you won't be imprisoned, stoned, or flogged this week for your faith as Paul was.

Still, contemporary society exerts subtle, psychological, daily pressures on you to turn your back on your faith and your values. Popular culture promotes promiscuity, atheism, and gutter language; your children's schools have kicked God out; the corporate culture advocates amorality before the shrine of the almighty dollar.

You have to hang tough to keep the faith.

Winning isn't imperative, but getting tougher in the fourth quarter is.
— Bear Bryant

Life demands more than mere physical toughness;
you must be spiritually tough too.

YOUNG BLOOD

Read: Jeremiah 1:4-10.

*"The Lord said to me, 'Do not say, 'I am only a child' . . .
for I am with you and will rescue you'" (vv. 7a, 8).*

As the Clemson athletic board considered who would succeed Charley Pell as head football coach in 1978, the favorite was an assistant named Danny Ford. The board had one major concern, though: Ford's youth.

Ford was only 30 years old when Pell bolted for Florida with a Gator-Bowl date against Ohio State only weeks away. Pell recommended that his young assistant replace him. Though Ford was only 23 games into his Clemson career, within 48 hours of Pell's leaving, the board made him the youngest Division I head coach in the country.

Ford understood the reservations about his youth and inexperience. "When the committee was interviewing me," he said, "the biggest item was my age. They talked about fear and awe. I told them, I don't fear anybody."

Ford had been even younger when he came to Clemson in 1977 and a newspaper article described him as the "highly retarded Danny Ford" rather than "highly regarded." When Ford asked if he could sue the paper, Bob Bradley, Clemson's Sports Information Director, replied, "Danny, you're gonna have to prove 'em wrong first."

After the disappointing 6-5 season of 1980, "ugly whispers

were heard about [Ford's] being too young to be a head coach." He knew that after only two full seasons of coaching, he "had reached a crossroad early in his career. He was aware he had to win and win big."

All Danny Ford did in 1981 was make his age forever irrelevant by becoming – at 33 -- the youngest head coach in NCAA football history to win the national championship.

While the media seem inordinately obsessed with youth, most aspects of our society value experience and some hard-won battle scars. Life usually requires us to spend time on the bench as a reserve, waiting for our chance to play with the big boys and girls. You probably rode some pine in high school. You started college as a lowly freshman. You began work at an entry-level position. Even head football coaches learn their trade as assistants.

Paying your dues is traditional, but that shouldn't stop you from doing something bold right away, as Danny Ford did. Nowhere is this truer than in your faith life.

You may well assert that you are too young and too inexperienced to really do anything for God. Those are just excuses, however, and God won't pay a lick of attention to them when he issues a call.

After all, the younger you are, the more time you have to serve.

You're only young once, but you can be immature forever.
                                    -- Former major leaguer Larry Andersen

**Youth is no excuse for not serving God;
it just gives you more time.**

DECIDE FOR YOURSELF

Read John 6:60-69.

"The words I have spoken to you are spirit and they are life. Yet there are some of you who do not believe" (vv. 63b-64a).

In 1951, Clemson athletic officials made a decision that changed to this day the face of Tiger athletics and eventually reshaped the landscape of college sports. They decided the football team should go to the Gator Bowl.

Clemson was then a member of the far-flung, 17-member Southern Conference, whose presidents, in an effort to de-emphasize football, recommended that the conference ban bowl trips by members that year.

After a 7-2 season, the Tigers received an invitation to play Miami in the Gator Bowl. In direct violation of the conference rule, the Tigers accepted. (Maryland made the same decision, playing in the Sugar Bowl.) On Dec. 15, the conference placed the two schools on probation, which meant no other conference member could play them in 1952.

"I just want everybody to know that I don't think it's right," Clemson coach Frank Howard declared after the meeting. "It was like I woke up this morning and found myself in Russia." Howard said "we knew we were in the wrong" to accept the bowl bid and that he came to Richmond to the meeting "to take our punishment like a man," but that tearing up the schedule was "a little bit harsher than we expected."

Howard managed to piece together a schedule for 1952 that included seven straight road games. The repercussions of the conference's ban on bowl bids climaxed on May 8, 1953, when seven schools – including Clemson -- withdrew from the Southern Conference and formed the Atlantic Coast Conference.

That defiant Clemson decision in 1951 changed the history of college athletics.

The decisions you made along the way shaped your life at every pivotal moment. Some decisions you made suddenly and frivolously; some – like Clemson's decision to play in the Gator Bowl -- you made carefully and deliberately; some were forced upon you. Perhaps decisions made for frivolous reasons have determined how your life unfolds, and you may have discovered that some of those spur-of-the-moment decisions have turned out better than your carefully considered ones.

Of all your life's decisions, however, none is more important than one you cannot ignore: What have you done with Jesus? Even in his time, people chose to follow Jesus or to reject him, and nothing has changed; the decision must still be made and nobody can make it for you. Carefully considered or spontaneous – how you arrive at a decision for Jesus doesn't matter; all that matters is that you get there.

If you make a decision that you think is the proper one at the time, then that's the correct decision.

-- *John Wooden*

**A decision for Jesus may be spontaneous or
considered; what counts is that you make it.**

DAY 15

A HOLLYWOOD ENDING

Read Luke 24:1-12.

"Why do you look for the living among the dead? He is not here; he has risen!" (vv. 5, 6a)

Even in Hollywood, the land of illusions, what happened on Oct. 10, 1992, might be considered too hokey for a screenplay.

Get the picture. No. 25 Clemson v. No. 10 Virginia up there. Virginia was simply slaughtering the Tigers, leading 28-0 in the second quarter. If that's not bad enough, the starting quarterback, Richard Moncrief, left the game late in the second quarter with an injury. Coach Ken Hatfield was forced to turn to a "puny (5-10, 168 pounds) redshirt freshman" named Louis Solomon who had played in only one college football game. Apparently, Solomon's mission was to avoid injury and keep the massacre from getting worse.

Hey, this is Hollywood. On his second series, Solomon went 64 yards for a touchdown. 28-7 at the half, and that play changed the whole game. "Louis was the spark," Hatfield said. "That was the play that turned it around."

In the last half, Solomon's perfect pitch let Rodney Blunt pick up 19 yards in a 63-yard touchdown drive. He hit Larry Ryans with a completion before a 53-yard TD run from Blunt. Then he scrambled for ten yards on fourth and five and went 13 yards on third and 10 to key another touchdown drive. That made it 28-26.

But there's more in Hollywood. With just over three minutes

left to play, Solomon delivered a strike to a wide-open Ryans for 45 yards to the Virginia nine. Four plays later, Nelson Welch kicked a field goal and the Tigers had a 29-28 win, the greatest comeback in school history.

Only a befuddled Hollywood script writer could come up with such an ending, right? Well, Hollywood and the Clemson Tigers.

The world tells us that happy endings are for fairy tales and the movies, that reality is Cinderella dying in childbirth and her prince getting killed in a peasant uprising. But that's just another of the world's lies.

The truth is that Jesus Christ has been producing happy endings for almost two millennia. That's because in Jesus lies the power to change and to rescue a life no matter how desperate the situation. Jesus is the master at putting shattered lives back together, of healing broken hearts and broken relationships, of resurrecting lost dreams.

And as for living happily ever after – God really means it. The greatest Hollywood ending of them all was written on a Sunday morning centuries ago when Jesus left a tomb and death behind. With faith in Jesus, your life can have that same ending. You live with God in peace, joy, and love – forever. The End.

This field, this game, is a part of our past, Ray. It reminds us of all that once was good, and that could be again.
-- James Earl Jones in Field of Dreams

Hollywood's happy endings are products of imagination; the happy endings Jesus produces are real and are yours for the asking.

DREAM WORLD

Read Joel 2:28-32.

"I will pour out my Spirit on all people. . . . Your old men will dream dreams" (v. 28).

Brittany Ross' dream of athletic stardom disappeared just as it was about to come true.

Ross was on track for a career that would make her one of the greatest volleyball players in Clemson history. She made the All-SEC freshman team in 2004 and was second-team All-ACC in 2005. The 2006 season was to be her break-out year. "We were all excited about what she would do this season," Clemson coach Jolene Hoover said.

Suddenly, though, it was all gone.

In May 2006, Ross collapsed while she was waiting in line for a flight home. "I started to feel very strange," she recalled. "I kept thinking it would go away, but the next thing I knew I woke up on the floor." Tests revealed a problem with her heart. "I had never been hurt in my whole career – from middle school through college," Ross said. "No sprains, no twisted ankles – nothing."

She couldn't imagine that the problem was serious, but it was. The top and bottom parts of her heart were not beating in sync, and various drug therapies failed to help. After one doctor suggested a pacemaker, Ross sought a second opinion. That cardiologist said he didn't want to put a pacemaker in a 20-year-old. She could live with the problem, even exercise, except that when she stopped jogging or training, she would pass out.

But the doctor also had some life-changing news: Ross could never play volleyball again. The dream was gone.

Ross cried on first hearing the fateful pronouncement, but then she left the bench for the bleachers and began using her story to point others to Christ. Rather than being devastated by the death of her dream, she stayed humble and obedient, her heart still beating for the one who made it.

Like Brittany Ross, we all have particular dreams. Perhaps to make a million dollars, write the Great American Novel, or find the perfect spouse. More likely than not, though, we gradually lose our hold on those dreams. They slip away from us as we surrender them to the reality of everyday living.

But we also have general dreams. For world peace. For an end to hunger. That no child should ever again be afraid. These dreams we hold doggedly onto as if something inside us tells us that even though the world gets itself into a bigger mess every year, one day everything will be all right.

That's because it will be. God has promised a time when his spirit will rule the world. Jesus spoke of a time when he will return to claim his kingdom. In that day, our dreams of peace and plenty and the banishment of hate and want will be reality.

Our dreams based on God's promises will come true.

To achieve in sports you first have to have a dream, and then you must act on that dream.

-- *Speed skater Dianne Holum*

Dreams based on God's promises will come true.

AT THE LAST TRUMPET

Read 1 Corinthians 15:50-58.

"The trumpet will sound, the dead will be raised imperishable, and we will be changed" (v. 52).

Football and academics weren't that all that hard for Kyle Young. Getting out of bed in the morning was a different matter.

Young was one of the greatest offensive linemen in Clemson history. He was All-America and All-ACC in both 2000 and 2001. A three-year letterman, he was a finalist as a junior and a senior for the Dave Rimington Award, presented to the nation's top center. He was a key figure in the Tigers' trips to three bowl games in Tommy Bowden's first three years, including the 2000 season when the Tigers finished 9-3 and were ranked 14th.

But Young was also one of the best students in Clemson football history. As a senior in 2001, he became the first Clemson football player in 23 years to win an NCAA Football Foundation Scholar Athlete Award. He won the Jim Tatum Award and the Anson Mount scholarship as the ACC's and the nation's top football scholar respectively. Young and golfer Jonathan Byrd are the only athletes in Clemson history to be named on-the-field and academic All-America twice. When Young was named Strength & Conditioning All-America in 2001, he became the only athlete in Clemson history to be named All-America in all three areas.

While Young pretty much overcame the challenges football and academics presented, he had a much tougher time with the alarm clock. When it went off, he had to get up, get dressed, and go eat. The coaches "require you to go to breakfast," Young moaned, noting that the cafeteria was only across the street. "But just getting out of bed is the toughest thing. [The coaches] make sure you're there. If you're not, you pay for it."

Life at Clemson was good for Kyle Young. The most challenging part of his day was showing up on time for bacon and eggs.

Being roused out of bed in the morning -- by a screaming alarm clock (one of life's most sadistic inventions) or by something a mite gentler -- may not be among the great joys of your life.

But one day you will be awakened by a trumpet shrieking in your ear – and you will be overjoyed about it. The Hebrew people of the Bible knew about the good news signaled by a trumpet blast because the sounding of the trumpets announced the start of the great festivals and other extraordinary events. Trumpets blown by the priests controlled and coordinated the march of the people to the Promised Land and reminded them that God watched over them.

The day will come when the last trumpet will sound in the final and true wake-up call. On that day, with that blast, Jesus will summon the faithful to paradise. No one – not even Kyle Young -- will ever need an alarm clock again.

He's a guy who gets up at six o'clock in the morning regardless of what time it is.

– Boxing trainer Lou Duva

**God will sound a final wake-up call
at which even the sleepiest will arise.**

THE GOOD OLD DAYS

Read Psalm 102.

"My days vanish like smoke; . . . but you remain the same, and your years will never end" (vv. 3, 27).

For many, the "good old days" of Clemson and ACC basketball are long gone, a different time, a different age "when players and coaches could beat each other's brains out and still be friends offcourt."

In those good old days, Clemson played in Fike Field House (from 1930 until Littlejohn Coliseum opened in 1968). "It was a different time back then," recalled Banks McFadden, a basketball All-America in 1939. (See devotion No. 51.) He conceded the game and the conditions for both fans and players have improved "maybe 10,000 times" since he played, but "relations were different then, too. It's a pleasant time to look back on."

For instance, Clemson basketball coach Press Maravich (1956-62) would always go out and eat with Wake Forest's legendary coach Horace "Bones" McKinney when the teams played each other. "The whole way of doing things was different back then," McKinney said. "You'd play two or three games at once against someone, and after the game, the players and coaches would eat at each other's place for dinner. . . . No matter who won, we were pretty good friends and what happened on the court wouldn't change that."

Frank Howard said the relationships were different in foot-

TIGERS

ball, too, in those good old days. He cited as evidence the 1971 funeral of "Peahead" Walker, longtime Wake Forest coach. The pallbearers included several football coaches, among them Bear Bryant, Bud Wilkinson of Oklahoma, Jim Tatum of Maryland, and Howard himself. "If a present ACC coach died tomorrow, it's highly doubtful that you'd find any of the other coaches being a pallbearer," Howard said.

But they were back in the "good old days" when relationships were very different from what they are today.

It's a brutal truth that time just never stands still. The current of your life sweeps you along until you realize one day you've lived long enough to have a past. Part of it you cling to fondly. The stunts you pulled with your high-school buddies. Your first apartment. That dance with your first love. That special vacation. Those "good old days."

You hold on relentlessly to the memory of those old, familiar ways because of the stability they provide in our uncertain world. They will always be there even as times change and you age.

Another constant exists in your life too. God has been a part of every event in your life that created a memory because he was there. He's always there with you; the question is whether you ignore him or make him a part of your day.

A "good old day" is any day shared with God.

Everything gets better as the years go by.

-- *Frank Howard*

**Today is one of the "good old days"
if you share it with God.**

RUN FOR IT

Read John 20:1-10.

"Peter and the other disciple started for the tomb. Both were running, but the other disciple outran Peter and reached the tomb first" (vv. 3-4).

Clemson track star Shawn Crawford has run some strange races in his life, but the strangest of all may have occurred in the 2008 Olympics.

From 1997-2000, Crawford ran for the Tigers. He was a three-time NCAA champion in the 200m dash and was an 11-time All-America, the most such honors in Clemson men's track and field history.

In January 2003 on a FOX episode of *Man vs. Beast*, Crawford raced both a zebra and a giraffe in a 100m dash on dirt. He easily beat the giraffe but lost to the zebra in a close race. He accused the zebra of a false start and ran the race again, but again was nipped at the finish line.

With a gold medal in the 200m dash and a silver medal in the 4x100m relay in the 2004 Olympics, Crawford became the only athlete with Clemson ties to win three Olympic medals when he won the silver in the 200m dash in Beijing in 2008.

But therein lies a tale. Crawford received that silver medal despite finishing fourth in the race, out-leaned at the finish line by an American teammate. Five minutes after the race was run, however, Crawford moved to third and the bronze medal when that teammate was disqualified for running out of his lane.

About an hour after that, the sprinter who had originally finished second was thrown out of the race for the same offense of running out his lane. Crawford wound up with the silver medal – "and a hollow feeling." "I didn't cross the line in second," he said. "And if I don't cross the line in second, I don't care if people are disqualified or not. I didn't deserve the medal."

Nevertheless, however strangely it may have happened, Shawn Crawford had run his way to a third Olympic medal.

Hit the ground running -- every morning that's what you do as you leave the house and re-enter the rat race. You run errands, you run though a presentation; you give someone a run for his money; you always want to be in the running and never run-of-the-mill.

You're always running toward something, such as your goals, or away from something, such as your past. Many of us spend much of our lives foolhardily attempting to run away from God, the purposes he has for us, and the blessings he is waiting to give us. No matter how hard or how far you run, though, you can never outrun yourself or God. God keeps pace with you, calling you in the short run to take care of the long run by falling to your knees and running for your life -- to Jesus -- just as Peter and the other disciple ran that first Easter morning.

On your knees, you run all the way to glory.

I never get tired of running. The ball ain't that heavy.
-- *Herschel Walker*

You can run to eternity by going to your knees.

HOME IMPROVEMENT

Read Hebrews 6:1-12.

"Let us go on towards perfection" (v. 1 NRSV).

Jess Neely had a recommendation for Frank Howard, his successor as Clemson's head football coach. Howard ignored it completely, and the result ultimately was one of the great showcases in college football.

Before Neely left for Rice after the 1939 season, he told Howard, "Don't ever let them talk you into building a big stadium. Put about 10,000 seats behind the YMCA. That's all you'll ever need."

When Howard took over, the team played at Riggs Field, which housed about 9,000. Building a big stadium did seem unfeasible, since Clemson played few home games each season anyhow.

But Neely was barely in Texas before Howard had plans for a new 20,000-seat stadium in a natural valley west of Riggs Field. Two members of the football team -- A.N. Cameron and Hugh Webb -- staked out the new stadium. With little mechanized equipment available, much of the dirt was moved by mules and a scoop.

On Sept. 19, 1942, Memorial Stadium opened for a 32-13 thrashing of Presbyterian – but just barely. As Howard put it, "The gates were hung at 1:00 and we played at 2:00."

But that was only the beginning. After World War II, crowds grew and so did Memorial Stadium. In 1958, 18,000 sideline seats were added; two end-zone expansions increased the capacity to 53,000. The south stands were double-decked in 1978, the north stands in 1983, which made the stadium one of the nation's largest on-campus facilities with a capacity of more than 80,000.

Today, the "storied edifice" that is Memorial Stadium is a special setting in which the Tigers prowl.

Great as it is, Memorial Stadium will always be subject to renovation and expansion to improve it. The same is true for our lives; they can always stand some improvement. It's not just the "New Year's Resolutions" improvements we need to make either; you know the kind: lose weight, be more punctual, spend more time with the kids. More important than those are the spiritual improvements we should be constantly making.

We can always know more about God's word, discover more ways to serve God, deepen our prayer life and our trust in God, and do a better job of being Jesus to other people through simple acts of kindness and caring.

We are always "under construction" as far as God is concerned because we are always striving toward spiritual perfection. We build constantly until the day we stand before God a finished product, presenting to him a spiritual mansion, not a hovel.

The principle is competing against yourself. It's about self-improvement, about being better than you were the day before.

-- Steve Young

**Renovation and sprucing up should be ongoing
for your body and your soul.**

ANGER MANAGEMENT

Read James 1:19-27.

"Everyone should be quick to listen, slow to speak and slow to become angry, for man's anger does not bring about the righteous life that God desires" (vv. 19-20).

One of the most famous plays in Clemson football history involved an opposing coach who lost his temper.

In 1978, Charley Pell's second year at the helm, the Tigers went 10-1 and were ranked seventh in the nation, won the ACC championship, and waxed South Carolina 41-23. They then accepted a bid to play Ohio State in the Gator Bowl.

Before the game, the news centered around Clemson's coach when Pell bolted for the University of Florida and assistant Danny Ford was named his successor. After the game, though, the story was Buckeye head man Woody Hayes.

Clemson led 10-9 at halftime behind a four-yard TD run by quarterback Steve Fuller, a field goal from Obed Ariri, and a blocked PAT. The Tigers went 84 yards in 19 plays in the third quarter, using up seven minutes. Freshman halfback Cliff Austin scored from the one, and Clemson led 17-9. State answered with a long drive of its own in the fourth quarter, but All-American lineman Jim Stuckey stopped the try for the two-point conversion. Clemson led 17-15.

A Tiger fumble late in the game gave Ohio State one last shot. On third and five at the Clemson 24, though, nose guard Charlie

Bauman intercepted a pass and went out of bounds in front of the Ohio State bench to clinch the Tiger win. In one of the most talked-about plays in the history of college football, Hayes went berserk and punched Bauman.

His temper cost Hayes, who had been coaching longer than Ford had been alive. Ohio State fired him the next day.

Our society today is well aware of anger's destructive power because too many of us – like Woody Hayes in Jacksonville -- don't manage our anger. Anger is a healthy component of a functional human being until – like other normal emotions such as fear, grief, and worry – it escalates out of control. Anger abounds when Clemson loses; the trouble comes when that anger intensifies from annoyance and disappointment to rage and destructive behavior.

Anger has both practical and spiritual consequences. Its great spiritual danger occurs when anger is "a purely selfish matter and the expression of a merely peevish vexation at unexpected and unwelcome misfortune or frustration" as when the Tigers fumble at the Gamecock five-yard line. It thus interferes with the living of the righteous, Christ-like life God intends for us.

Our own anger, therefore, can incur God's wrath; making God angry can never be anything but a perfectly horrendous idea.

When you get angry and start shouting, nothing good ever really happens.

--Olympic rower Michelle Guerette

**Anger becomes a problem when it escalates
into rage and interferes with the righteous life
God intends for us.**

STAR POWER

Read Luke 10:1-3, 17-20.

"The Lord appointed seventy-two others and sent them two by two ahead of him to every town and place where he was about to go" (v. 1).

With its tradition of success, the Clemson women's basketball program has had its share of stars, but the greatest of them all never had a basketball scholarship.

Among Clemson's stars, All-ACC guard Amy Geren (1995-99) defeated the men's three-point shooting champion, Jason Terry, in a "Battle of the Sexes" on national TV in 1999. All-American forward Jessica Barr (1992-94) was the first Lady Tiger to be named the ACC Player of the Year (1994). Center Erin Batth (1997-2001) was the first Clemson player to be drafted by the WNBA. Guard Itoro Umoh (1995-99) was the unanimous MVP of the 1999 ACC Tournament; she went on to play in the 2004 Olympic Games. Shandy Bryan, Mary Anne Cubelic, Umoh, Geren, and Janet Knight have all been inducted into the Clemson Athletic Hall of Fame.

And then there's Barbara Kennedy (1978-82), the first women's basketball player to be inducted into the Ring of Honor. It's been said of her that she "set the standard for all Lady Tigers on and off the court."

She still holds the school and the conference records for most points scored and most rebounds in a career. She holds school and conference season records for most points, points per game

(29.3), most field goals, rebounds, and rebounds per game (12.9). She was All-America in 1981 and '82, and first-team All-ACC three times, the only athlete in Clemson history to be so honored. She still holds the NCAA record for most field goals in a season.

And this star, who was named Clemson's top athlete of the 1980s, came to Clemson on a volleyball scholarship because Coach Annie Tribble had no basketball scholarships left.

Basketball teams are like other organizations in that they may have a star like Barbara Kennedy but the star would be nothing without the supporting cast. It's the same in a private company, in a government bureaucracy, in a military unit, and just about any other team of people with a common goal.

That includes the team known as a church. It may have its "star" in the preacher, who is – like the quarterback or the company CEO – the most visible representative of the team. Preachers are, after all, God's paid, trained professionals.

But when Jesus assembled a team of seventy-two folks, he didn't have anybody on the payroll or any seminary graduates. All he had were no-names who loved him. And nothing has changed. God's church still depends on those whose only pay is the satisfaction of serving and whose only qualification is their love for God. God's church needs you.

You may have the greatest bunch of individual stars in the world, but if they don't play together, the club won't be worth a dime.
– Babe Ruth

Yes, the church needs its professional clergy,
but it also needs those who serve as volunteers
because they love God; the church needs you.

THE FUNERAL

Read Romans 6:3-11.

"If we died with Christ, we believe that we will also live with him" (v. 8).

The Baron of Barlow Bend got quite a sendoff.

Millionaires, school employees, and farm boys; dignitaries such as a U.S. senator, football coaches, athletic directors, television personalities, and former football players -- on Jan. 28, 1996, they all gathered on Cemetery Hill overlooking Memorial Stadium for the funeral of Frank Howard. Tears mingled with chuckles at the graveside services of Clemson's winningest football coach, who led the Tigers from 1940 to 1969. Howard had purchased a particular cemetery plot so, he said, he could spend all eternity there, "listening to the cheers for my Tigers" as they played and won on the field that bears his name.

Though it was a bright Sunday afternoon, the lights were on inside the stadium and the scoreboard read "Frank Howard 1909-1996." The Rev. Joe Bowen, a former player, said that "many found their best, truest and strongest self under Coach Howard." The Rev. Charlie Horne, also a former Howard player, thanked God "that your plan for the world included Frank Howard."

The service's music included "Rock of Ages," a not-so-subtle reference to Howard's Rock. After a slide show that was a montage of Howard's life, the mourners sang the Clemson alma mater. On the last line, they raised their right hands and waved as Tiger alums always do, only this time they were waving good-bye to their great friend. A respectful silence settled over the group until suddenly the Clemson pep band struck up "Tiger Rag," and everybody clapped along.

As one writer put it, "Frank Howard was Clemson." And Clemson on that sad, sunny day said good-bye.

You may not get that kind of send-off, one usually reserved for the likes of politicians, business bigwigs, local legends, and some college football coaches. Still, you want a good funeral. You want a decent crowd, you want folks to shed some tears, and you want some reasonably distinguished-looking types to stand behind a lectern and say some very nice things about you. Especially if they're all true.

But have you ever been to a funeral where the deceased you knew and the deceased folks were talking about were two different people? Where everyone struggled to say something nice about the not-so-dearly departed? Or a funeral that was little more than an empty acknowledgement that death is the end of all hope. Sad, isn't it?

Exactly what does make a good funeral, one where people laugh, love, and remember warmly and sincerely amid their tears? Jesus does. His presence transforms a mourning of death into a celebration of life.

Always go to other people's funerals; otherwise, they won't come to yours.

-- Yogi Berra

Amid tears there is hope; amid death there is resurrection – if Jesus is at the funeral.

DAY 24

HEAD GAMES

Read Job 28.

"The fear of the Lord -- that is wisdom, and to shun evil is understanding" (v. 28).

Frank Howard used logic to get one of Clemson's best football players ever into the lineup.

Shad Bryant was "shunned by other schools because of his smallness," but he played at Clemson from 1937-39 at both wingback and safety. He remains Clemson's career leader in punt return yards, was All-Southern Conference in 1939, and was inducted into the Clemson Hall of Fame in 1979.

Perhaps because of his size, Coach Jess Neely was reluctant to use Bryant in 1938 except in spot situations. South Carolina had a scatback about Bryant's size named Al Grygo. As Big Thursday neared, Neely approached Howard, who had scouted Carolina, and asked him if Grygo were better than Shad. Howard's reply was blunt: "Yes, sir."

Neely didn't like that answer, so he proceeded to get particular and got particular answers. "Is Grygo faster than Shad?" "No, sir." "Is he a better runner?" "Naw." Is he a better punt returner?" "Naw." "Is he a better defensive safety man?" "He ain't near as good." "Can he run the reverse as well?" "Naw."

By this time, Neely was thoroughly confused and downright vexed, noting that Howard had declared that Grygo was better than Shad while claiming Shad could do everything better than his Carolina counterpart. "I don't think you've got good sense," Neely fulminated.

Then Howard delivered his carefully planned clincher. "I'll tell you how it is," he said. "They're playing Grygo 60 minutes of every game and we're only playing Shad about five. I figured Grygo must be better."

Thanks to Howard's undeniable logic, Shad started the next game and was a regular from then on.

You're a thinking person. When you talk about using your head, you're speaking as Frank Howard demonstrated when discussing Shad Bryant: Logic and reason are part of your psyche. A coach's bad call frustrates you and your children's inexplicable behavior flummoxes you. Why can't people just think things through?

That goes for matters of faith, too. Jesus doesn't tell you to turn your brain off when you walk into a church or open the Bible. In fact, when you seek Jesus, you seek him heart, soul, body, and mind. The mind of the master should be the master of your mind so that you consider every situation in your life through the critical lens of the mind of Christ. With your head *and* your heart, you encounter God, who is, after all, the true source of wisdom.

To know Jesus is not to stop thinking; it is to start thinking divinely.

Football is more mental than physical, no matter how it looks from the stands.

-- *Pro Hall-of-Fame linebacker Ray Nitschke*

**Since God is the source of all wisdom,
it's only logical that you encounter him
with your mind as well as your emotions.**

DAY 25

THOSE THINGS

Read Isaiah 55:6-13.

"For my thoughts are not your thoughts, neither are your ways my ways" (v. 8).

Kevin Hines never saw it coming, and it ended his basketball career.

"It" was the elbow of a Georgia Tech player on the night of Feb. 4, 1993. A senior forward, Hines remembered little about the inadvertent blow to the head that knocked him unconscious and sent him to Atlanta's Piedmont Hospital. When a nurse told him he was in Piedmont, Hines thought of the former airline and asked, "Why have y'all got me on a plane?" He thought team physician Stuart Clarkson was head trainer Reno Wilson and kept calling him Reno. When Wilson arrived and Clarkson called him Reno, a confused Hines asked, "There are two Renos now?"

At first the doctors told him he would miss at least two weeks. On February 18, though, Hines got the unexpected news that he shouldn't play anymore. After he talked it over with his mother, he decided to trust the doctor's decision. His next concern was for his teammates, who expected him to return. He called Coach Cliff Ellis and told him he wanted to tell the guys.

In considering what to say, Hines began with his strong faith in God. He told the team his injury "was a case of God using me. . . . I told them I was going to be all right, that God was going to make everything all right. And I asked them to pray for me." He

TIGERS

didn't leave a dry eye in the house.

Honored with the other seniors on March 7, Hines couldn't stay for the game, coincidentally against Georgia Tech. The bright lights and the noise still triggered headaches, dizziness, and blurred vision.

Kevin Hines' life-changing injury was just one of those things.

You've probably had a few of "those things" in your own life: bad breaks that occur without regard to justice, morality, or fair play. You wonder if everything in life is random with events determined by a chance roll of some cosmic dice. Is there really somebody scripting all this with logic and purpose?

Yes, there is; God is the author of everything.

We know how it all began; we even know how it all will end. It's in God's book. The part we play in God's kingdom, though, is in the middle, and that part is still being written. God is the author, and his ways are different from ours. After all he's God and we are not. That's why we don't know what's coming our way, and why "those things" catch us by surprise and dismay us when they do occur.

What God asks of us is that we trust him. He knows everything will be all right for those who follow Jesus.

Sometimes the calls go your way, and sometimes they don't.
-- Olympic gold medalist Dr. Dot Richardson

**Life confounds us because, while we know the
end and the beginning of God's great story, we are
part of the middle, which God is still unfolding.**

STRANGE BUT TRUE

Read 1 Corinthians 1:18-31.

"The message of the cross is foolishness to those who are perishing, but to us who are being saved it is the power of God" (v. 18).

It's strange but true: A jump off a diving board in Mississippi netted Frank Howard what he called "probably the best, if not the best, football player" he ever had, a youngster who never played a down of high school football.

Fred Cone played for Clemson from 1948-50 and led the Tigers to two undefeated seasons and two bowl games. His senior season he set school records with 845 yards rushing and 15 touchdowns. He also set school career records in both categories. He went on to play for the Green Bay Packers and was inducted into their Hall of Fame in 1974. In 1997, he was the fourth Clemson football player to be inducted into the Football Ring of Honor.

Cone's strange odyssey to Clemson and football began when he visited his sister in Biloxi. She lived next door to Frank Howard's sister, who wrote her brother, "I have you a good football player, but he's never played football." Howard had told the school registrar to save him forty beds in the barracks, and at the time he had only 39 names on the list. So he simply wrote in Fred Cone as the 40th name.

So how in the world did Howard's sister -- whom Sports Information Director Bob Bradley said Howard should have named his recruiting coordinator -- know Cone would make such a great football player? Even Howard couldn't figure that one out. But it was very simple. On that fateful visit Cone made in 1946, she had seen him jump off a diving board "and he just looked so athletic."

And so Fred Cone's journey to Clemson remains the strangest recruiting story in school history.

Life is just strange, isn't it? How else to explain the college bowl situation, Dr. Phil, tattoos, curling, tofu, and teenagers? Isn't it strange that today we have more ways to stay in touch with each other yet are losing the intimacy of personal contact?

And how strange is it that God let himself be killed by being nailed to a couple of pieces of wood? Think about that: the creator and ruler of the entire universe suffering the indignity and the torture that he did. And he did it quite willingly; this was God, after all. It's not like he wasn't capable of changing the course of events -- but he didn't. Isn't that strange?

But there's more that's downright bewildering. The cross, a symbol of disgrace, defeat, and death, ultimately became a world-wide symbol of hope, victory, and life. That's really strange.

So is the fact that love drove God to that cross. It's strange – but it's true.

It may sound strange, but many champions are made champions by setbacks.
                                        -- Olympic champion Bob Richards

It's strange but true: God allowed himself to be killed on a cross because of his great love for you.

DAY 27

TOLD YOU SO

Read Matthew 24:15-31.

"See, I have told you ahead of time" (v. 25).

Clemson told them ahead of time; Illinois would have done well to listen.

The week before the Hall of Fame Bowl of Jan. 1, 1991, Clemson's defensive players wore T-shirts that proclaimed "No. 1 defense in the nation." They were bragging, but they also were telling the simple truth. Yielding 216.9 yards per game, the Tiger defense was the best in college football.

Their opponent, Illinois, disparaged that claim. "They said we hadn't played many Top 10 teams, that we'd lost to the only two we'd played," said linebacker Ed McDaniel. Coach Ken Hatfield repeatedly read to his players a newspaper article that "talked about how we played such [a] wienie schedule in the ACC."

Illinois didn't have much to say at game's end, though, after a 30-0 mauling in which the Tiger defense "dominated," even "negated" Illinois' supposedly powerful offense.

On Illinois' first play, McDaniel caused a fumble that linebacker John Johnson recovered to set up the first Tiger touchdown. Four possessions later, linebacker Levon Kirkland pressured the Illinois quarterback into an interception that rover Arlington Nunn returned for a touchdown.

But wait, there's more. Linebacker Chuck O'Brien intercepted

TIGERS

a pass tipped by Kirkland. Doug Brewster blocked a punt. When Illinois got a chance to avert a shutout from the Clemson six, tackle Chester McGlockton caused a fumble that McDaniel recovered.

Defensive coordinator Bob Trott had said the Clemson defense had to be "like sharks, smell the blood and pour it on." Bob Gillespie wrote, "Illinois didn't have a lifeguard's chance."

But they should have seen it coming; Clemson told them so. All they had to do was read the T-shirts.

Don't you just hate it in when somebody says, "I told you so"? That means the other person was right and you were wrong; that other person has spoken the truth. You could have listened to that know-it-all in the first place, but then you would have lost the chance yourself to crow, "I told you so."

In our pluralistic age and society, many view truth as relative, meaning absolute truth does not exist. All belief systems have equal value and merit. But this is a ghastly, dangerous fallacy because it ignores the truth that God proclaimed in the presence and words of Jesus.

In speaking the truth, Jesus told everybody exactly what he was going to do: come back and take his faithful with him. Those who don't listen or who don't believe will be left behind with those four awful words, "I told you so," ringing in their ears and wringing their souls.

There's nothing in this world more instinctively abhorrent to me than finding myself in agreement with my fellow humans.
-- *Lou Holtz*

**Jesus matter-of-factly told us what he has planned:
He will return to gather all the faithful to himself.**

LESSON LEARNED

Read Matthew 11:20-30.

"Take my yoke upon you and learn from me" (v. 29).

Gary Burnham's freshman baseball season ended after only fifteen games when he tore his anterior cruciate ligament in a collision with a Clemson teammate. He profited from the down time, though, using it not just to rehab but also to learn a valuable lesson about life.

Burnham's immediate reaction to the devastating injury was the remorseful cry, "Not again." He had suffered the same injury in high school. This time, though, Burnham knew the territory. "I knew exactly what to do," he said. "I knew what feelings to expect along the way." So he not only rehabbed physically but psychologically too. He returned to the lineup as a sophomore with a valuable lesson learned from months spent sitting and watching others play the game he loved: That each day is valuable and life should be fun.

"Every day, I come out and run," Burnham said. "I thank the Lord that that's another day I'm out here having a good time, because for two years out of my life I've spent rehabbing and watching everyone else have fun."

Burnham wound up having a lot of fun at Clemson before he finished. In 1995, he batted .344 and led the team with 27 doubles. The Tigers were 54-14, advanced to the College World Series, and finished #6 in the nation. In '96, Burnham batted .290 and led the 51-17 and 5th-ranked Tigers in doubles as the team again made it to the CWS. His senior season, Burnham batted a hefty .391 and led the team with 104 hits and 82 RBIs.

"You look at life differently after you've been in the cellar health-wise," Burham said during his sophomore season. Lesson learned.

Learning about anything in life requires a combination of education and experience. Education is the accumulation of facts that we call knowledge; experience is the acquisition of wisdom and discernment, which add purpose and understanding to our knowledge.

The most difficult way to learn is trial and error: dive in blindly and mess up. The best way to learn is through example coupled with a set of instructions: Someone has gone ahead to show you the way and then written down all the information you need to follow.

In teaching us the way to live godly lives, God chose the latter method. He set down in his book the habits, actions, and attitudes that make for a way of life in accordance with his wishes. He also sent us Jesus to explain and to illustrate.

God teaches us not only how to exist but also how to live. We just need to be attentive students.

It's what you learn after you know it all that counts.

— *John Wooden*

To learn from Jesus is to learn what life is all about and how God means for us to live it.

DAY 29

NAME DROPPING

Read Exodus 3:13-20.

"God said to Moses, 'I AM WHO I AM. This is what you are to say to the Israelites: 'I AM has sent me to you'" (v. 14).

Running back Lester "Rubber Duck" Brown. The Baron of Barlow Bend, aka Frank Howard. James "Mutt" Gee, a center who later became Clemson's athletic director. And then there's Dumb Dumb Wyndham, blessed -- or cursed -- with perhaps the most colorful nickname in Clemson history.

Steven Friendly Wyndham was an All-South star, a blocking back on offense and a linebacker on defense for Howard's 1948-50 teams. He was inducted into the Clemson Hall of Fame in 1980. Howard dubbed him "Dumb Dumb" because of his tendency to go the wrong way on offense. To this day, though, Wyndham remains one of the hardest hitting linebackers in Tiger history.

In Clemson's 34-0 shellacking of Missouri in 1950, Wyndham's tackles knocked three Missouri players out of the game. Finally in desperation, the Missouri captain pleaded with the referee, telling him if he didn't "get that wild man out of there, he's going to kill [us] all."

Jackie Calvert went 81 yards on the first play from scrimmage to begin the rout against the 18th-ranked Tigers from Missouri. With the game well in hand, Howard began to substitute freely. Wyndham finally trotted over to Howard and said, "Coach, how about not putting more than six of them sorry ones in on defense with me at one time. I can protect six of them, but I don't think I can protect more than six." Howard responded by letting "Dumb Dumb" Wyndham be in charge of substitutions after that as long as he got everybody into the game.

Nicknames such as "Dumb Dumb" may not accurately reflect a person's character or qualities, but they usually are not slapped haphazardly upon individuals. Rather, they reflect widely held perceptions about the person named. Proper names do that also.

Nowhere throughout history has this concept been more prevalent that in the Bible, where a name is not a mere label but is an expression of the essential nature of the named one. That is, a person's name reveals his or her character. Even God shares this concept; to know the name of God is to know God as he has chosen to reveal himself to us.

What does your name say about you? Honest, trustworthy, a seeker of the truth and a person of God? Or does the mention of your name cause your coworkers to whisper snide remarks, your neighbors to roll their eyes, or your friends to start making allowances for you?

Most importantly, what does your name say about you to God? He, too, knows you by name.

A good nickname inspires awe and ensures that you'll be enshrined in the Pantheon of [Sports] Legends.

-- Funny Sports Quotes blog

**Live so that your name evokes
positive associations by people you know,
the public, and God.**

THE FAME GAME

Read 1 Kings 10:1-10, 18-29.

"King Solomon was greater in riches and wisdom than all the other kings of the earth. The whole world sought audience with Solomon" (vv. 23-24).

The most famous play in Clemson football history was one quarterback Homer Jordan and wide receiver Perry Tuttle made up.

In the 1982 Orange Bowl, the top-ranked Tigers led Nebraska only 12-7 in the third quarter when they drove to a first down at the Nebraska four. A botched pitch on second down, though, moved the ball back to the 13.

Often at practice when they weren't running through drills, Jordan and Tuttle had made up plays. Repeatedly, on their own, they had practiced a fade route. Jordan told his receiver, "Tut, if I ever nod my head, just run to the corner." Now as the team huddled for one of the most crucial plays in Clemson's long football history, Jordan told Tuttle to be ready. Then he called another play and they broke the huddle.

Jordan surveyed the defense and saw that Tuttle had drawn single coverage. He nodded; the fade was coming. Tuttle understood and ran to the corner; Jordan threw what Tuttle described as "a perfect strike, a great ball to catch." "I just laid it up, and he went and got it," Jordan said.

Tuttle's touchdown catch was immortalized when it appeared on the cover of *Sports Illustrated*, the only one ever to feature a

Clemson athlete in action. The catch and the photo made Tuttle "a hero forever to the Tigers faithful, hundreds of whom sent him copies of the issue to autograph." More than twenty years later, Tuttle still signed copies of that magazine. "Where are they coming from?" he asked in wonder.

Have you ever wanted to be famous? Hanging out with other rich and famous people, having folks with microphones listen to what you say, throwing money around like toilet paper, meeting adoring and clamoring fans, signing autographs like Perry Tuttle, and posing for the paparazzi?

Many of us yearn to be famous, well-known in the places and by the people that we believe matter. That's all fame amounts to: strangers knowing your name and your face.

The truth is that you are already famous where it really does matter, which excludes TV's talking heads, screaming teen-agers, moviegoers, or D.C. power brokers. You are famous because Almighty God knows your name, your face, and everything ·about you.

If a persistent photographer snapped you pondering this fame – the only kind that has eternal significance – would the picture show the world unbridled joy or the shell-shocked expression of a mug shot?

Fame is fleeting. As soon as I play poorly, you guys will be interviewing somebody else.

-- NFL quarterback Tony Romo

You're already famous because God knows your name and your face, which may be either reassuring or terrifying.

DAY 31

MIRACLE PLAY

Read Matthew 12:38-42.

"He answered, 'A wicked and adulterous generation asks for a miraculous sign!'" (v. 39)

College sports in general and Clemson in particular have seen some incredible moments, but the performance of the 1987 Clemson men's soccer team "rivals any miracle in NCAA sports."

In August, Coach I.M. Ibrahim said that for his club "the national championship was not a realistic goal." This was a stark admission from the coach whose team in 1984 had won the title.

The team certainly didn't make a liar out of its coach during the regular season, struggling to a 1-4-1 record in ACC play. "Few thought Clemson would be invited to the big dance," but they were, reportedly receiving the 23rd invitation in the 24-team field.

Shipped off to Evansville, IN, the Tigers beat the host team 2-1 in the first round and then stunned top-ranked Indiana 2-1, again getting the winner on a last-half goal by Bruce Murray. Clemson next beat Rutgers 3-2 with goalkeeper Tim Genovese making a save on a penalty kick with less than two minutes left to play.

That win not only sent the Tigers into the final four, but it resulted in their being awarded the home site. The miracle run continued with a 4-1 rout of North Carolina, which had beaten Clemson twice in the regular season. Freshman Pearse Tormey scored two goals before more than 6,500 wildly cheering fans.

The Tigers met San Diego State in the finals and won 2-0,

getting a first-half goal from Paul Rutenis and clinching the national championship with a goal from Richie Richmond with just 41 seconds left.

"I dreamed about this earlier in the season," Ibrahim said, "but quite honestly I did not think we could win the championship." That was before his team made its miracle run.

Miracles defy rational explanation. Like sweeping through the field for a national championship after a shaky season. Or escaping with minor abrasions from an accident that totals your car. Or recovering from an illness that seemed terminal. Underlying the notion of miracles is that they are rare instances of direct divine intervention that reveal God.

But life shows us quite the contrary, that miracles are anything but rare. Since God made the world and everything in it, everything around you is miraculous. Even you are a miracle. Your life can be mundane, dull, and ordinary, or it can be spent in a glorious attitude of childlike wonder and awe. It depends on whether or not you see the world through the eyes of faith; only through faith can you discern the hand of God in any event. Only through faith can you see the miraculous and thus see God.

Jesus knew that miracles don't produce faith, but rather faith produces miracles.

Do you believe in miracles? Yes!
– Broadcaster Al Michaels when U.S. defeated USSR in hockey in 1980
Winter Games.

Miracles are all around us,
but it takes the eyes of faith to see them.

FATHER FIGURE

Read Matthew 3:13-17.

"A voice from heaven said, 'This is my Son, whom I love; with him I am well pleased'" (v. 17).

Clemson was on its own 32, trailing South Carolina 14-13 with only 59 seconds left to play. Death Valley was a frenzied mess, except for the Tiger quarterback, junior Woody Dantzler, who was quite calm. After all, his dad was there.

From 1998-2001, Dantzler set 52 school, conference, and NCAA records. He was the first quarterback in NCAA history to pass for 5,000 yards and rush for 2,500 yards. While Charlie Whitehurst (2002-05) eclipsed many of Dantzler's passing records, he is still responsible for more touchdowns – 68, 27 rushing and 41 passing – than any player in Tiger history. Clemson's top three single greatest offensive performances in a game are all Dantzler's.

At no time did Dantzler demonstrate his poise under pressure more than in that 2000 South Carolina game – but he had some help. As he stepped into the huddle, he looked over at Section C where his father was cheering wildly. His dad's presence had always brought Dantzler "a sense of peace, so when he stepped into the huddle, he told his teammates, 'Losing this game is not about to happen.'"

It didn't. On third and twelve from the Tiger 42, Dantzler fired a strike to senior receiver Rod Gardner at the Gamecock eight with ten seconds left. Freshman Aaron Hunt kicked the game-winning field goal from there. 16-14 Clemson.

Asked after the game if he were scared of losing, Dantzler laughed in reply. He knew real fear most of his life because his dad had for years battled a rare and deadly blood disorder. "I've gathered strength," Dantzler said, from watching his father fight.

American society largely belittles and marginalizes fathers and their influence upon their sons. Men are perceived as necessary to effect pregnancy; after that, they can leave and everybody's better off.

But we need look in only two places to appreciate the enormity of that misconception: our jails – packed with males who lacked the influence of fathers in their lives as they grew up -- and the Bible. God – being God – could have chosen any relationship he desired between Jesus and himself, including society's approach of irrelevancy. Instead, the most important relationship in all of history was that of father-son.

God obviously believes a close, loving relationship between fathers and sons, such as that of Woody Dantzler and his dad, is crucial. For men and women to espouse otherwise or for men to walk blithely and carelessly out of their children's lives consti-tutes disobedience to the divine will.

Simply put, God loves fathers. After all, he is one.

My dad was a huge influence on me. I imagine if he had put a wrench in my hand I would have been a great mechanic.
                                                              -- Pete Maravich

**Fatherhood is a tough job, but a model
for the father-child relationship is found
in that of Jesus the Son with God the Father.**

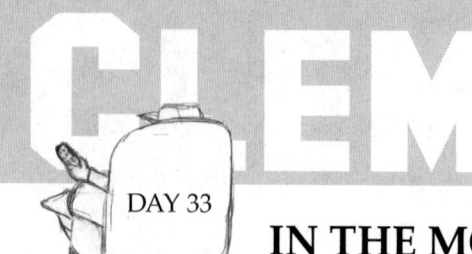

IN THE MONEY

Read Luke 16:1-15.

"You cannot serve both God and money" (v. 13b).

One of the quaintest aspects of Frank Howard's tenure as head football coach at Clemson is that he had only one contract his entire career – and he lost that one.

Howard spent 39 years at Clemson as a coach, thirty of them as the head man. After the 1939 season, head coach Jess Neely left for Rice. The athletic council met to pick a successor, and Howard sat quietly in the back of the room, having been asked to be present for policy discussions.

The council was apparently much aware of the contributions Howard had made to the athletic program. Professor S.R. "Slim" Rhodes nominated Howard as athletic director and head coach. A voice from the back of the room suddenly said, "I second that motion." Frank Howard had seconded his own nomination. The board took it from there.

He originally received a four-year contract, but he misplaced it on a business trip. After that, an annual handshake with the college president formalized the deal. He never received another written contract.

The president who originally hired Howard told him he didn't want his coach going around telling everyone how much money he made. Howard replied, "You don't need to worry none 'cause

I'm ashamed of it as you are."

When Howard asked a later president about a raise, he was told he couldn't get a raise, but he could get some "titles and degrees." "Doc, you know those titles and degrees are fine," Howard retorted, "but they don't educate kids, and they don't put groceries on the table." He didn't get the raise, though.

Having a little too much money at the end of the month may be as bothersome -- if not as worrisome -- as having a little too much month at the end of the money. The investment possibilities are bewildering: stocks, bonds, mutual funds, that group pooling their money to open up a neighborhood coffee shop -- that's a good idea.

You take your money seriously, as well you should. Jesus, too, took money seriously, warning us frequently of its dangers. Money itself is not evil; its peril lies in the ease with which it can usurp God's rightful place as the master of our lives.

Certainly in our age and society, we often measure people by how much money they have. But like our other talents, gifts, and resources, money should primarily be used for God's purposes. God's love must touch not only our hearts but our wallets also.

How much of your wealth are you investing with God?

Money can buy you everything but happiness. It can pay your fare to everywhere but heaven.

-- Pete Maravich

**Your attitude about money says much
about your attitude toward God.**

DAY 34

HERO WORSHIP

Read 1 Samuel 16:1-13.

"Do not consider his appearance or his height, for . . . the Lord does not look at the things man looks at. . . . The Lord looks at the heart" (v. 7).

One of the all-time great untold stories."

That's what Clemson starting point guard Bobby Conrad called the story of the night in 1979 when an unlikely hero helped the Tigers defeat North Carolina.

With 54 seconds to play, 11-5 Clemson led 14-2 UNC when Marvin Dickerson drove to the basket, drew a foul, and came up holding a wrist. Coach Bill Foster pointed to a substitute to go in and shoot the crucial one-and-one free throws, and the capacity crowd gasped in surprise.

David Poole had walked on the Clemson football team until an injury ended his career. At the time, Foster had only nine returning players and no scholarships because of sanctions left over from the previous coach. So his coaches had scoured the gyms for intramural players and had found Poole, who turned out to be good enough to remain on the squad after the scholarships returned.

In 1979, Poole had played only seven minutes in the season's first sixteen games. Nevertheless, he was the one Foster chose to come off the bench cold and shoot what could be two of the most important free throws in school basketball history. Foster knew

TIGERS

something, however, that the stunned and fretting crowd did not: In the Tigers' year-long free-throw competition in practice, Poole led the team.

The player Conrad called "Cool Poole" coolly made both free throws, and Clemson had a win over North Carolina. "What he did is remarkable," Conrad said. "Not many players could do that, coming off the bench like that with so much pressure and making those foul shots."

For one night, David Poole was a Clemson Tiger hero.

A hero is commonly thought of as someone who performs brave and dangerous feats that save or protect someone's life or someone who comes through under intense pressure as David Poole did. You figure that excludes you.

But ask your son about that when you show him how to bait a hook, or your daughter when you show up for her dance recital. Look into the eyes of those Little Leaguers you help coach.

Ask God about heroism when you're steady in your faith. For God, a hero is a person with the heart of a servant. And if a hero is a servant who acts to save other's lives, then the greatest hero of all is Jesus Christ.

God seeks heroes today, those who will proclaim the name of their hero – Jesus – proudly and boldly, no matter how others may scoff or ridicule. God knows heroes when he sees them -- by what's in their hearts.

Heroes and cowards feel exactly the same fear; heroes just act differently.
-- Boxing trainer Cus D'Amato

**God's heroes are those who remain steady
in their faith while serving others.**

FAMILY TIES

Read Mark 3:31-35.

"[Jesus] said, 'Here are my mother and my brothers! Whoever does God's will is my brother and sister and mother'" (vv. 34-35).

Clemson has had some brother combinations play football for them over the years, but few of them had a family life quite as interesting as Chuck and Rod McSwain.

On the national championship team of 1981, Chuck was a junior tailback who split time with Cliff Austin, and Rod was a sophomore cornerback who was the top backup. Chuck was the ACC Rookie-of-the-Year in 1979; Rod was All-ACC as a senior. Both brothers went on to play in the NFL.

The McSwain brothers were two of thirteen children raised in a three-bedroom house in North Carolina. Preparations for bedtime each night included pulling out roll-away beds that had been tucked under the main beds in the bedrooms. Chuck recalled, "I always tell the story that, when I was growing up, I never fell out of a bed. You could roll from one bed to another all the way across the room." Chuck also declared that when the family "would go out to eat, you'd get one order of fries or get one hamburger. You didn't get both."

Because the McSwains were such a large family and didn't have a vehicle big enough for them all, they rarely traveled far. The Orange-Bowl trip in 1981 was Chuck's first trip to the beach though he lived only five hours from Myrtle Beach. Even after he decided to commit to Clemson because he liked the small-town atmosphere and the country manners of Coach Danny Ford, Chuck made trips to Georgia Tech and Notre Dame because he wanted to fly, which he had never done before.

Rod chose Clemson because his brother was there, and they decided to room together, inseparable family members.

Some wit said families are like fudge, mostly sweet with a few nuts. You can probably call the names of your sweetest relatives, whom you cherish, and of the nutty ones too, whom you mostly try to avoid at a family reunion.

Like it or not, you have a family, and that's God's doing. God cherishes the family so much that he chose to live in one as a son, a brother, and a cousin.

One of Jesus' more startling actions was to redefine the family. No longer is it a single household of blood relatives or even a clan or a tribe. Jesus' family is the result not of an accident of birth but rather a conscious choice. All those who do God's will are members of Jesus' family.

What a startling and wonderful thought! You have family members out there you don't even know who stand ready to love you just because you're part of God's family.

Football has affected my entire family's lifestyle. My little boy can't go to bed unless we give him a two-minute warning.
-- Former NFL coach Dick Vermeil

For followers of Jesus, family comes not from a shared ancestry but from a shared faith.

SMART MOVE

Read 1 Kings 4:29-34; 11:1-6.

"[Solomon] was wiser than any other man. . . . As Solomon grew old, his wives turned his heart after other gods, and his heart was not fully devoted to the Lord his God" (vv. 4:31, 11:4).

A smart move tricked the Seminoles, and the result was a Clemson win.

On Sept. 16, 2006, the Tigers and the ninth-ranked Noles were locked up at 20 as the clock wound down to one minute. Clemson sat at its own 49 with a first and ten looking for all the world as though it would play for overtime; that's when the Tigers made their move. It "was a call we had talked about at halftime," said offensive coordinator Rob Spence. "It's just a quick, easy call."

The key was "quick." For most of the game, Clemson ran its offense without a huddle. The offense trudged up to the line of scrimmage, stopped, and waited for Spence to signal a play in to quarterback Will Proctor. Correspondingly, the FSU defense stood and waited for a signal from its defensive coordinator. So as time ran out, nobody on the Seminole side was expecting anything different -- but they got it.

This time when the offense walked to the line, the center snapped the ball without waiting for a signal from Spence. Proctor handed off to running back James Davis, who bolted for the side-line. "I didn't really know we were going to quick snap it," Davis said. "We saw them standing and looking to their side of the field for a call. I was to the corner before they were set."

He was also way down the field before the startled Seminoles could catch him. Forty-seven yards later, Davis went down at the four. On third down, he scored, and Clemson had a 27-20 win on a trick play that was simply a smart move.

Remember that time you wrecked the car when you spilled hot coffee on your lap? That cold morning you fell out of the boat? The time you gave your honey a tool box for her birthday?

Formal education notwithstanding, we all make some dumb moves sometime because time spent in a classroom is not an accurate gauge of common sense. Folks impressed with their own smarts often grace us with erudite pronouncements that we intuitively recognize as flawed, unworkable, or simply wrong.

A good example is the observation that great intelligence and scholarship are not compatible with faith in God. That is, the more we know, the less we believe. But any incompatibility occurs only because we begin to trust in our own wisdom rather than the wisdom of God. We forget, as Solomon did, that God is the ultimate source of all our knowledge and wisdom and that even our ability to learn is a gift from God.

Not smart at all.

I don't hire anybody not brighter than I am. If they're not smarter than me, I don't need them.

-- *Bear Bryant*

**Being truly smart means trusting in God's
wisdom rather than only in our own knowledge.**

FRUIT TREES

Read Matthew 7:15-20.

"By their fruit you will recognize them" (v. 20).

Fruit once played a role in one of the biggest maulings Clemson ever laid on another football team.

On Oct. 10, 1903, the Tigers began their season with a 29-0 whipping of Georgia. Next on the schedule was Georgia Tech. Even back then the hatred between the Georgia rivals was so strong that the Bulldog players sought a way to get at Tech through Clemson. They cooked up a deal with the Carolina boys by offering them anything they wanted for every point over 29 by which they beat Tech. The Tigers wanted apples.

The haughty *Atlanta Journal* sniffed, "Eating applies is said to be the crowning dissipation of the Clemson student body. The town itself has not yet been incorporated on the map and such vicious habits as demon rum, ping pong, and other forms of vice common to the large city are unknown." The paper went on, "No sooner is school dismissed than the collegians rush to the apple granary and feed on the succulent fruit as a pastime. Now Clemson's orchards are bare and apples are what the boys want most."

Clemson's brilliant left end, Vet Sitton, was injured, so "Tech officials displayed guarded optimism" about the Oct. 17 game. They shouldn't have. Clemson coach John Heisman had a more-than-able substitute in Gil Ellison, who was not as fast as Sitton but who was bigger and stronger. He led the Tigers to a 73-0 slaughter of the Atlanta boys, a margin of victory that remains the fifth largest in Clemson football history.

That score sent the Athens boys to scrambling, but they managed to round up forty-four bushels of "select, rosey apples, booked at $1 per bushel" and ship them to the Clemson players.

Strawberry shortcake. Apple pie. Ice-cold watermelon. Banana pudding. Straight up, congealed, or served with whipped cream or ice cream, fresh fruit is hard to beat. We even use it symbolically to represent the good things in our lives: A promotion or a raise is the fruit of our good work.

Fruity metaphors and images conjure up thoughts of something sweet and satisfying. Little in life, however, is as rancid as fruit gone bad. That dual image of fruit at its best and its worst is what Jesus had in mind when he spoke of knowing both false prophets and faithful followers by their fruit.

Our lives as disciples of Jesus should yield not just material fruits but spiritual fruits also. Our spiritual fruits are what we leave in our wake: heartbreak, tears, anger, bitterness, and dissension; or peace, love, joy, generosity, and gentleness.

Good or bad – delicious or rotten -- these are the fruits by which we shall be known by those around us – and by God.

On these fields of friendly strife are sown the seeds that on other fields, and other days, will bear the fruits of victory.
-- Gen. Douglas MacArthur on athletic competition

God knows you by your spiritual fruits, not the material ones the world fancies so.

SEEING THE VISION

Read Acts 26:1, 9-23.

"So then, . . . I was not disobedient to the vision from heaven" (v. 19).

One of Bill McLellan's visions played such an important role in the 1982 Orange Bowl that Nebraska head coach Tom Osborne said it was the difference in the game.

McLellan succeeded Frank Howard, for whom he played from 1952-54, as athletic director in 1971. Current Clemson athletic director Terry Don Phillips labeled him "a visionary." Coach Danny Ford agreed, declaring, McLellan "had great foresight."

Under McLellan's watch, the Jervey Athletic Center office complex was constructed, and Memorial Stadium was renovated more than once. He was an innovative leader, among the first in the country to create luxury boxes at a college stadium. His addition of the upper decks at the stadium became the model for other universities. He oversaw improvements in the baseball, track, soccer, swimming, and tennis facilities and helped IPTAY grow into the number-one fundraising organization in the country. "He just had great vision," Ford said.

Among his visions was that of a world-class weight facility. In 1976, he hired the late George Dostal, a coach and master motivator, to build it. He effectively gave Dostal a blank check. Like his boss, Dostal was a visionary, ahead of his time in his emphasis on stretching and cross training.

TIGERS

One of the Nebraska coaches watched Clemson's players get off the bus before the 1982 Orange Bowl and told Dostal his players were too tall and skinny. "Yours are awful short and fat," Dostal replied.

After Clemson's win, Osborne told Dostal, "I've never played against a team that had players in such good condition. You deserve all the credit for what happened here."

It was just part of Bill McLellan's vision.

To speak of visions is often to risk their being lumped with palm readings, Ouija boards, seances, horoscopes, and other such useless mumbo-jumbo. The danger such mild amusements pose, however, is very real in that they indicate a reliance on something other than God. It is God who knows the future; it is God who has a vision and a plan for your life.

You probably do have a vision for your life, a plan for how it should unfold. It's the dream you pursue through your family, your job, your hobbies, your interests. But your vision inspires a fruitful life only if it is compatible with God's plan. As the apostle Paul found out, you ignore God's vision at your peril. But if you pursue it, you'll find an even more glorious life than you could ever have envisioned for yourself.

If I could see into the future, I wouldn't be sitting here talking to you doorknobs. I'd be out investing in the stock market.
-- Boston Celtic Kevin McHale to reporters

Your grandest vision for the future
pales beside the vision God has
of what the two of you can accomplish together.

DAY 39

FAITHFUL LIVES

Read Hebrews 11:1-12.

"Faith is the substance of things hoped for, the evidence of things not seen" (v. 1 NKJV).

When Tommy Bowden coached the Tigers, the faithful knew they had a Christian man at the helm. Nothing changed when Dabo Swinney became Clemson's 25th head football coach on Dec. 1, 2008.

"I'm a Christian and very proud of that," Swinney said. "I am who I am. That isn't going to change." Swinney understands, though, that he is a coach at a public institution. "My job is to win games. My job is not to save [the football players]. . . . I do think it's my job to provide opportunities for young men to grow in every area as they choose." And that includes spiritually.

The frank spirituality of the Clemson coaches certainly had an effect on the 2009 recruiting class. Several new Tigers said that Swinney's Christianity and that of his coaches played a part in their decision to play for Clemson. Safety Jonathan Meeks said the coaches' openness about their faith changed his mind. "It shocked me because I wasn't planning on going to Clemson," he said.

Bryce McNeal, a wide receiver from Minneapolis, said, "One thing that really sold me and my parents was that all [the Clemson] coaches are mainly Christians and strong believers and practice it."

TIGERS

Swinney said the frank discussion of faith by the coaches isn't something that comes up to press prospects, but rather it arises naturally as the players and their families want to know more about the coaches. When folks ask a personal question, Swinney said, they get a personal answer.

More often than not, that personal answer includes a declaration of faith in Jesus Christ.

As with the Clemson coaches, your faith forms the heart and soul of what you are. Faith in people, things, ideologies, and concepts to a large extent determines how you spend your life. You believe in the Tigers, in your family, in the basic goodness of Americans, in freedom and liberty, and in abiding by the law. These beliefs mold you and make you the person you are.

This is all great stuff, of course, that makes for decent human beings and productive lives. None of it, however, is as important as what you believe about Jesus. To have faith in Jesus is to believe his message of hope and salvation as recorded in the Bible. True faith in Jesus, however, has an additional component; it must also include a personal commitment to him. In other words, you don't just believe in Jesus; you live for him.

Faith in Jesus does more than shape your life; it determines your eternity.

To me, religion – faith – is the only real thing in life.
                                                            -- Bobby Bowden

Your belief system is the foundation upon which you build a life; faith in Jesus is the foundation for your eternal life.

DAY 40

AMAZING!

Read: Luke 4:31-36.

"All the people were amazed and said to each other, 'What is this teaching? With authority and power he gives orders to evil spirits and they come out!'" (v. 36)

Clemson's highly successful baseball program has given its fans many amazing moments, but nothing can top what may well be the most incredible comeback in college baseball history.

Amazing can well describe many moments in Tiger baseball history. For instance, in 1946 Joe Landrum pitched a no-hitter in his first collegiate appearance. Bill Wilhelm coached the Tigers for 36 years and never had a losing season. Clemson scored 19 runs in the third inning against Maryland in 1998; the Tigers didn't score another run. They also scored 18 runs in the ninth inning in an amazing 41-9 whipping of N.C. State in 1979.

But then there is what happened on April 14, 1995.

In the first of a three-game set, N.C. State scored three in the seventh and six in the eighth to blow open a close game and lead 15-4 headed into the top of the ninth. The first Tiger batter struck out. Then came something for the ages.

Clemson got three hits and two walks before a fielder's choice recorded the second out and cut the lead to 15-7. Then the next six Tigers rapped out hits, including a three-run homer by Shane Monahan that made it 15-13. Two more hits and a walk preceded a double by Matthew LeCroy that tied the game. Trailing 15-4 on

TIGERS

the road, the Tigers had scored 11 runs in the ninth inning, all after one out, eight of them after two outs, and all without benefit of a single Wolfpack error.

They then won the most amazing game in Clemson baseball history 17-15 in ten innings.

The word *amazing* defines the limits of what you believe to be plausible or usual. The Grand Canyon, the birth of your children, those last-gasp Clemson comebacks that snatch victory from sure defeat -- they're amazing! You've never seen anything like that before!

Some people in Galilee felt the same way when they encountered Jesus. Jesus amazed them with the authority of his teaching, and he wowed them with his power over spirit beings. People everywhere just couldn't quit talking about him.

It would have been amazing had they not been amazed. They were, after all, witnesses to the most amazing spectacle in the history of the world: God himself was right there among them walking, talking, teaching, preaching, and healing.

Their amazement should be a part of your life too because Jesus still lives. The almighty and omnipotent God of the universe seeks to spend time with you every day – because he loves you. Amazing!

It's amazing. Some of the greatest characteristics of being a winning football player are the same ones it's true to be a Christian man.
-- Bobby Bowden

**Everything about God is amazing,
but perhaps most amazing of all is that he loves us
and desires our company.**

AS A RULE

Read Luke 5:27-32.

*"Why do you eat and drink with tax collectors and
'sinners'?" (v. 30b)*

Frank Howard once had second thoughts about kicking three
players off the team for rules violations, so he made sure they got
reinstated in time for the Orange Bowl.

The Tigers stayed at the now-defunct Flamingo Motel on the
beach when they went to Miami for the 1952 Orange Bowl, and
Howard instituted some stringent curfew rules, ordering the
players to be in their rooms every night by 10:30. One night at
bed check, he discovered three players missing and waited up
on them until 1:30 when they came sneaking in. "Howard gave
them a verbal whiplashing that probably still rings in their ears,"
including his pronouncement that "they were too sorry to play
with [his] good boys." He then told them he was sending them
back to Clemson in the morning on the bus.

The problem was that the three were not "too sorry"; they were
blocking back Don Wade, end Glenn Smith, and fullback Fred
Cone, three of the team's best players. Howard quickly began
to rethink his extreme punishment: "I got to thinking to myself
that maybe I'd got into this too deep." So he searched about for a
way to have the trio play in the Orange Bowl while not eroding
his authority over the team. He decided to let the team vote on
whether or not the penitent miscreants should play. Before the

vote, though, Howard told assistant coach Bob Jones to do some politicking with the players to make sure they voted "right."

They did, all three played, and Smith tackled a Miami back in the end zone late in the game for the difference in the 15-14 Clemson win.

You live by rules others set up. Some lender determined the interest rate on your mortgage and your car loan. You work hours and shifts somebody else established. Someone else decided what day your garbage gets picked up and what school district your house is in.

Jesus encountered societal rules also, including a strict set of religious edicts that dictated what company he should keep, what people, in other words, were fit for him to socialize with, talk to, or share a meal with. Jesus ignored the rules, choosing love instead of mindless obedience and demonstrating his disdain for society's rules by mingling with the outcasts, the lowlifes, the poor, and the misfits.

You, too, have to choose when you find yourself in the presence of someone whom society deems undesirable. Will you choose the rules or love? Are you willing to be a rebel for love — as Jesus was?

I believe in rules. Sure I do. If there weren't any rules, how could you break them?

-- Leo Durocher

**Society's rules dictate who is acceptable
and who is not, but love in the name of Jesus
knows no such distinctions.**

WINNING

Read 1 John 5:1-12.

"Who is it that overcomes the world? Only he who believes that Jesus is the Son of God" (v. 5).

There is winning, and then there is what the Clemson men's basketball team did to Duke on Feb. 4, 2009.

Before a national television audience and a raucous capacity crowd at Littlejohn Coliseum the 10th-ranked Tigers simply slaughtered the No. 4 Blue Devils 74-47. That's 27 points, the worst defeat for Duke in nine years. Duke's Mike Krzyzewski summed up the whipping: "There wasn't momentum. It was 40 minutes of dominating. . . . We had no chance of winning this game. None."

The win was perhaps the biggest of yet another great basketball season. The Tigers went 23-9 in 2008-09, the fifth highest win total in school history and the third straight season they had won at least 20 games. They finished the season ranked 24th and joined Duke and North Carolina as the only ACC schools to make the NCAA Tournament for the second straight season.

Junior forward Travis Booker, who led the conference in field goal percentage and rebounding for the season, effected the most carnage against Duke with 21 points and eight rebounds. Sophomore guard Terrence Oglesby had 17 points, and senior guard K.C. Rivers added eleven points and seven rebounds and tied the school record with seven steals.

But a stunning display by the Tiger defense was what really

TIGERS

turned the game into a rout. In experiencing their worst shooting night of the season, the Blue Devils' pitiful 47-point total was the second-lowest output in Krzyzewski's 29 seasons at Duke.

Littlejohn was rocking and rocking, and Coach Oliver Purnell said his Tigers "were ready for this atmosphere. . . . [We] just kind of rode the crowd as the game went along."

All the way to a season-defining win.

Life itself, not just athletic events, is a competition. You vie against all the other job or college applicants. You compete against others for a date. Sibling rivalry is real; just ask your brother or sister.

Inherent in any competition or any situation in which you strive to win is the involvement of an antagonist. You always have an opponent to overcome, even if it's an inanimate video game, a golf course, or even yourself.

Nobody wants to be numbered among life's losers. We recognize them when we see them, and maybe mutter a prayer that says something like, "There but for the grace of God go I."

But one adversary will defeat us: Death will claim us all. We *can* turn the tables on this foe, though; we *can* defeat the grave. A victory is possible, however, only through faith in Jesus Christ. With Jesus, we have hope beyond death because we have life.

With Jesus, we win. For all of eternity.

I love the winning. I can take losing, but most of all, I love to play.
-- Tennis great Boris Becker

Death is the ultimate opponent;
Jesus is the ultimate victor.

FOOD FOR THOUGHT

Read Genesis 9:1-7.

"Everything that lives and moves will be food for you. Just as I gave you the green plants, I now give you everything" (v. 3).

He's not fat fat. He's just hungry."

So spoke Coach Danny Ford about one of Clemson's greatest and most beloved football players ever: William "The Refrigerator" Perry.

A freshman on the 1981 national championship team, "The Fridge" came to Clemson weighing 285 pounds. And got bigger. He was a three-time All American and three-time All-ACC middle guard (1982-84) who in 2003 was named one of the 50 greatest male athletes in ACC history. Perry's athletic ability plus his massive size made him a phenomenon.

He came by his size courtesy of genetics and food. Perry Tuttle and Jeff Davis were his player hosts on his recruiting visit in 1980, and they took him to a local pizza parlor where he ordered two large pizzas. "I thought he was pretty bold to order for all of us," Tuttle said. But then Perry asked them what they were having. They watched in wonder as he devoured both pizzas, taking two slices at a time and folding them together like a sandwich.

His sophomore season Perry showed up overweight, and the coaches told him to eat some bananas, figuring this would load him up with simple sugars he could burn off quickly. Dan Benish, who would go on to play defensive tackle in the NFL, arrived in the dining hall and saw Perry's tray piled high with bananas. "You couldn't get any more banana peels on that tray," Benish said. "He took every banana that was on the fruit tray and ate every single one of them."

William "The Refrigerator" Perry was indeed a storehouse for food.

Belly up to the buffet, boys and girls, for barbecue, sirloin steak, grilled chicken, and fried catfish with hush puppies. Rachael Ray's a household name; hamburger joints, pizza parlors, and taco stands lurk on every corner; and we have a TV channel devoted exclusively to food. We love our chow.

Food is one of God's really good ideas, but consider the complex divine plan that gets those French fries to your mouth. The creator of all life devised a system in which living things are sustained and nourished physically through the sacrifice of other living things in a way similar to what Christ underwent to save you spiritually. Whether it's fast food or home-cooked, everything you eat is a gift from God secured through a divine plan in which some plants and animals have given up their lives.

Pausing to give thanks before you dive in seems the least you can do.

I really ain't much of an after-dinner speaker. I'm just after a dinner and I don't mind talking for it.
-- Frank Howard

God created a system that nourishes you through the sacrifice of other living things; that's worth a thank-you.

CHANCE MEETING

Read Luke 24:13-35.

*"That same day two of them were going to a village. . . .
They were talking with each other about everything that
had happened. . . . Jesus himself came up and walked
along with them" (vv. 13-15).*

Dwight Clark's life and career changed forever because he did his roommate a favor and showed up at a meeting that wasn't about him at all.

Charley Pell's Tiger teams of 1977 and 1978 were loaded with stars. Offensive guard Joe Bostic was All-America in 1977, and quarterback Steve Fuller was the ACC Player of the Year. Jonathan Brooks, Lacy Brumley, Jerry Butler, Steve Ryan, and Randy Scott joined Fuller and Bostic on the All-ACC team. Six players from the 1978 team would eventually be first-round NFL draft picks: Fuller, Butler, Jim Stuckey, Jeff Bryant, Perry Tuttle, and Terry Kinard.

Clark, the player on those two teams who went on to become one of the greatest pros in history, wasn't among those stars. In fact, his shot at a pro career resulted from a visit by San Francisco 49er coach Bill Walsh to see Fuller work out. According to Clark, Walsh – looking for Fuller -- called the dorm room they shared and Clark answered the phone. When Walsh learned whom he was speaking to and that he was a receiver, he asked Clark to help him test Fuller's arm by running some routes. Clark obliged.

Walsh eventually drafted Clark in the tenth round. Clark went on to an All-Pro career that included the most famous catch in NFL playoff history, the snare in the end zone from Joe Montana that defeated Dallas in 1982, a play subsequently known as "The Catch." The 49ers later retired Clark's jersey number.

All because he showed up at a meeting to help his roommate.

Maybe you met your spouse in the frozen food section of a supermarket. Perhaps a conversation in an elevator led to a job offer. Or maybe – like Dwight Clark – you were incidental to a meeting that changed the direction of your life.

Chance meetings often shape our lives, but some meetings are too important to be left to what seem like the whims of life. If your child is sick, you don't wait until you happen to bump into a physician at Starbuck's to seek help.

So it is with Jesus. Too much is at stake to leave a meeting with him to chance. Instead, you intentionally seek him at church, in the pages of your Bible, on your knees in prayer, or through a conversation with a friend or neighbor. How you conduct the search doesn't matter; what matters is that you find him.

Once you've met him, the acquaintance should then be intentionally cultivated until it is a deep, abiding, life-shaping and life-changing friendship.

If you think it's hard to meet new people, try picking up the wrong golf ball.

-- Jack Lemmon

A meeting with Jesus should not be a chance encounter, but instead should be sought out.

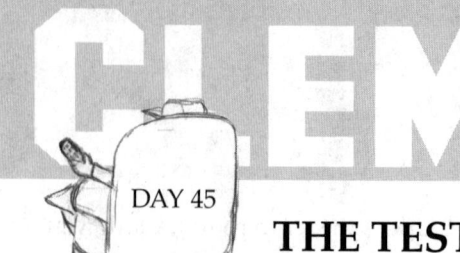

DAY 45

THE TESTING TIME

Read James 1:2-12.

"Blessed is the man who perseveres under trial, because when he has stood the test, he will receive the crown of life that God has promised to those who love him" (v. 12).

Cris Robinson just couldn't pass the test.

Chuck Kriese is the winningest men's tennis coach in ACC history both in total wins and conference matches. He took over the Clemson program in 1975 and turned it into a national power-house. Dedication and discipline are the basics of his coaching philosophy. His training methods include Morning Madness, which is two weeks of running at 6 a.m. with a 5:15 mile required to make the team.

Cris Robinson failed eight times in 1991 to make that 5:15 time. He had excuses: He was short, only 5'7", and he was a diabetic. Kriese considered making an exception in Robinson's case, but he realized that "on the court and in the world, Cris would not just be competing against small diabetics." So he reaffirmed to Robinson that the 5:15 time was the only way he could make the team. Robinson agreed to try one last time.

Kriese used a ball of kite string and two upperclassmen as pacers. He tied fifteen feet of string around the waist of each pacer and told Robinson, "When you're at the end of your rope, tie a knot and hang on." Each pacer ran two laps. When the string got taut as Robinson's pace slowed, Kriese screamed, "No!" in encouragement.

As Robinson fell across the finish line, the coach's stopwatch read 5:11. Kriese "coyote-howled and laughed outrageously and ran with Robinson on his victory lap with the string in hand."

His test passed, Cris Robinson went on to win six titles in 1994 and 1995 and was the MVP of the 1995 team that made it to the NCAA semifinals.

Life often seems to be just one battery of tests after another: high-school and college final exams, college entrance exams, the driver's license test, professional certification exams. They all stress us out because they measure our competency, and we fear that we will be found wanting.

But it is the tests in our lives that don't involve paper and pen that often demand the most of us. That is, like Cris Robinson's battle with the time trial, we regularly run headlong into challenges, obstacles, and barriers that test our abilities, our faith, and our persistence.

Life itself is one long test, which means some parts are bound to be hard. Viewing life as an ongoing exam may help you keep your sanity, your perspective, and your faith when troubles come your way. After all, God is the proctor, but he isn't neutral. He even gave you the answer you need to pass with flying colors; that answer is "Jesus."

Experience is a hard teacher because she gives the test first, the lesson afterward.

-- Former major league pitcher Vernon Law

Life is a test that God wants you to ace.

CALLING IT QUITS

Read Numbers 13:25-14:4.

"The men who had gone up with him said, 'We can't attack those people; they are stronger than we are'" (v. 13:31).

The most storied running back in Clemson football history was ready to quit before his college career ever really started – until his mother straightened him out.

From 1994-97, Raymond Priester ran the football as nobody else in Tiger history has. He still holds eighteen school records, including most yards rushing in a career (3.966), most yards rushing in a season (1,345 in 1996), and most yards rushing in a game (263 vs. Duke in 1995).

Priester chose Clemson out of high school expressly because Coach Rick Stockstill promised him he could play running back. When he arrived on campus, however, Priester met the reality of big-time college football: The Tigers had some very good running backs already on hand. Three games into his freshman season Priester had carried the ball one time. He was ready to quit the team and transfer.

First, though, he figured he'd better check with his mother. Her answer was absolute and to the point. "No, you're not," she said. "You're going to work it out." She went on to tell her son "he was going to stay right there and wait his turn. You don't play by yourself. You play as a team."

TIGERS

Even while his mother was making sure Priester would never again consider quitting, events transpired to change his life and Clemson football history. Staring at a 1-2 record, first-year Tiger coach Tommy West wanted to shake things up. Priester was a shakee. He started the next game, rushing for 88 yards on 19 carries and scoring his first collegiate touchdown in a 13-0 win over Maryland.

After that, Raymond Priester would quit running only when he had used up his eligibility.

Remember that time you quit a high-school sports team? Bailed out of a relationship? Walked away from that job with the goals unachieved? Sometimes quitting is the most sensible way to minimize your losses, so you may well at times in your life give up on something or someone.

In your relationship with God, however, you should remember the people of Israel, who quit when the Promised Land was theirs for the taking. They forgot one fact of life you never should: God never gives up on you. That means you should never, ever give up on God. No matter how tired or discouraged you get, no matter that it seems your prayers aren't getting through to God, no matter what – quitting on God is not an option. He is preparing a blessing for you, and in his time, he will bring it to fruition -- if you don't quit on him.

The first time you quit, it's hard. The second time, it gets easier. The third time, you don't even have to think about it.

-- Bear Bryant

Whatever else you give up on in your life, don't give up on God; he will never ever give up on you.

CHEAP TRICKS

Read Acts 19:11-20.

"The evil spirit answered them, 'Jesus I know, and I know about Paul, but who are you?'" (v. 15)

One of the most successful tricks ever pulled by a Clemson football coach on an opponent was managed by John Heisman against Georgia Tech – before the game even began.

With some creative camouflage in 1902, Heisman instilled the Tech players with such overconfidence that they failed to get serious about the game. The contest in Atlanta was billed as the Country Bumpkins against the City Slickers. Thus, the city boys and their fans were quite delighted when the Clemson team arrived and showed a "scrawny, anything-but-tough physical appearance."

The Clemson players "checked into their rooming houses and immediately started dispersing to all of the Atlanta nightspots for a real country-come-to-town festival." The hospitable Tech folks helped the Tigers enjoy their night out "by buying them mugs of beer, providing them with dancing partners and generally helping them make a big evening of it."

The game was in the bag, since obviously nobody could play good football the day after such a night of carousing. Except that the Tigers crushed Tech 44-5. How in the world could anyone be so hardy?

They couldn't. Heisman had rounded up some willing cadets

and sent them into Atlanta with instructions to party hearty "but be sure to enjoy yourself so the Tech team can't help but hear about it." Meanwhile, the real football players were sequestered at the railroad stop of Lula, a few miles north of Atlanta, and arrived in town on game day "as fresh as the dew 'where the Blue Ridge yawns its greatness.'"

The country bumpkins had tricked the city slickers but good.

Scam artists are everywhere — and they love tricks and trick plays. An e-mail encourages you to send money to some foreign country to get rich. That guy at your front door offers to resurface your driveway at a ridiculously low price. A TV ad promises a pill to help you lose weight without diet or exercise.

You've been around; you check things out before deciding. The same approach is necessary with spiritual matters, too, because false religions and bogus Christian denominations abound. The key is what any group does with Jesus. Is he the son of God, the ruler of the universe, and the only way to salvation? If not, then what the group espouses is something other than the true Word of God.

The good news about Jesus does indeed sound too good to be true. But the only catch is that there is no catch. No trick -- just the truth.

When you run trick plays and they work, you're a genius. But when they don't work, folks question your sanity.

-- Bobby Bowden

God's promises through Jesus sound too good to be true, but the only catch is that there is no catch.

DAY 48

TOP SECRET

Read Romans 2:1-16.

"This will take place on the day when God will judge men's secrets through Jesus Christ, as my gospel declares" (v. 16).

Center Terry Berryhill did his best to keep his secret, but his fellow linemen learned it anyway.

The offensive linemen on Clemson's 1981 national champions were quite practiced in what seems to be a universal trait for the men in the trenches: They were pranksters. They even had a particular brand of insanity they called "it-ing." Before practice, they would meet to watch film, turn off the lights, and immediately begin what they called "it sessions," "playfully trying to drive one another nuts."

They took particular delight in insulting each other's mothers. What seemed like a harmless way to keep each other loose and laughing actually became useful on the field. The linemen often had to change their blocking calls during a game because defensive players would quickly figure out what the calls meant. Thus, the linemen would create new calls, some real and others mere dummy calls that meant nothing and served to distract the defense. The linemen of 1981 often used their knowledge of each other's mothers' names for those calls. The favorite was "Mazell," guard James Farr's mom.

Berryhill was among the instigators of the motherly humor,

but he kept his own mother out of it by keeping her name a secret. In an age before the Internet and databases, he told her never to give her name out over the phone to anyone who asked for it.

One day, though, guard Brian Butcher stunned Berryhill by asking him, "How's Celia doing?" While Berryhill's mother had followed his advice, a resourceful Butcher had called Berryhill's grandmother. The center's secret was out.

Like Terry Berryhill's attempt to keep his mother's name a secret, we have to be vigilant about the personal information we prefer to keep secret. Much information about us—from credit reports to what movies we rent—is readily available to prying and persistent persons. In our information age, people we don't know may know a lot about us — or at least they can find out. And some of them may use this information for harm.

While diligence may allow us to be reasonably successful in keeping some secrets from the world at large, we should never deceive ourselves into believing we are keeping secrets from God. God knows everything about us, including the things we wouldn't want proclaimed at church. All our sins, mistakes, failures, shortcomings, quirks, prejudices, and desires – God knows all our would-be secrets.

But here's something God hasn't keep a secret: No matter what he knows about us, he loves us still.

The secret of winning is working more as a team, less as individuals.
— Knute Rockne

We have no secrets before God, and it's no secret that he nevertheless loves us still.

DAY 49

THE PIONEER SPIRIT

Read Luke 5:1-11.

"So they pulled their boats up on shore, left everything and followed him" (v. 11).

What a few buddies at Clemson started in 1931 culminated in 2003 when the Tiger golf team won the national championship.

Alan Johnstone was a junior when he and some pals decided they wanted to form a college golf team. They went to the office of the athletics director, J.G. "Mutt" Gee, and asked for his blessing. "You can have a golf team," he told them, "but I can't finance it."

So that's how it started: no scholarships, no eye-catching orange shirts with Tiger paws on them, no golf bags. The pioneering team included Johnstone, Charlie Moss, Tom Dashiell, Richie Ramseur, William Hicks, and a player identified in the yearbook only as Cohen. The coach was a volunteer, the Rev. G.H. Hodges. That first team finished 3-3 with a pair of wins over Presbyterian and a split with Furman. "We all had our own clubs, and we'd practice our driving at [Clemson's] dairy farm," Johnstone remembered.

Johnstone was the last surviving member of that team in 2003 when Coach Larry Penley's top-ranked Tigers won the national championship, becoming the first team in NCAA history to win its conference, the NCAA regional, and the national title in the same year. D.J. Trahan, Jack Ferguson, Matt Hendrix, Gregg Jones, and Ben Duncan were the aces that edged Oklahoma State by two strokes on the Cowboys' home course for the title.

TIGERS

Before the 2003 season began, Penley named Johnstone an honorary team captain, thanking him "for paving the way for the tradition and heritage we have established over the years." Asked about blazing a trail for an eventual national champion, Johnstone laughed. "We didn't think of it in that light," he said. "We just wanted to have a golf team."

Going to a place in your life you've never been before requires a willingness to take risks and face uncertainty head-on. You may have never helped start a new sports program at a major college, but you've had your moments when your latent pioneer spirit manifested itself. That time you changed careers, ran a marathon, volunteered at a homeless shelter, learned Spanish, or went back to school.

While attempting new things invariably begets apprehension, the truth is that when life becomes too comfortable and too familiar, it gets boring. The same is true of God, who is downright dangerous because he calls us to be anything but comfortable as we serve him. He summons us to continually blaze new trails in our faith life, to follow him no matter what. Stepping out on faith is risky all right, but the reward is a life of accomplishment, adventure, and joy that cannot be equaled anywhere else.

Life is an adventure. I wouldn't want to know what's going to happen next.
-- Bobby Bowden

Unsafe and downright dangerous, God calls us out of the place where we are comfortable to a life of adventure and trailblazing in his name.

DANCING MACHINE

Read 2 Samuel 6:12-22.

"David danced before the Lord with all his might, while he and the entire house of Israel brought up the ark of the Lord with shouts and the sound of trumpets" (vv. 14-15).

Steve Fuller showed some moves on the field as a Clemson quarterback, but he also shuffled his way to a part in the most famous football video ever made.

Fuller started 27 consecutive games for the Tigers in the late 1970s. He was All-ACC in both 1977 and '78 and was a third-team All-America in 1978 when he led Clemson to an 11-1 season that included an ACC championship and a No. 6 final ranking. He was the ACC Player of the Year in both 1977 and '78 and was the second athlete in Clemson history to have his jersey number retired. He was inducted into the Clemson Hall of Fame in 1985 and the Ring of Honor in 1994.

Fuller went on to a ten-year NFL career. In 1984, he was a free agent and decided to sign with the Chicago Bears as a backup to Jim McMahon. Fuller had his short-lived song-and-dance career in Chicago when some of the Bears decided to record a video prior to the 1986 Super Bowl against New England. The result was the infamous "Super Bowl Shuffle."

Ten players – including legendary running back Walton Payton, McMahon, and linebacker Mike Singleton – participated with the anchor of the ensemble being Clemson's own rookie tackle

TIGERS

William "The Refrigerator" Perry. Fuller got into the act because of his roommate on the road, receiver Willie Gault.

The Shuffle reached No. 41 on the *Billboard* charts and earned a Grammy nomination. "It was fun," Fuller recalled, "but we all say, 'Thank goodness we won, or we never would've lived it down.'" The Bears, including Fuller, danced their way to a 46-10 rout of the Patriots in Super Bowl XX.

One of the more enduring stereotypes of the Christian is of a dour, sour-faced person always on the prowl to sniff out fun and frivolity and shut it down. "Somewhere, sometime, somebody's having fun – and it's got to stop!" Many understand this to be the mandate that governs the Christian life.

But nothing could be further from reality. Long ago King David, he who numbered Jesus Christ among his house and lineage, set the standard for those who love and worship the Lord when he danced in the presence of God with unrestrained joy. Many centuries and one savior later, David's example today reminds us that a life spent in an awareness of God's presence is all about celebrating, rejoicing, and enjoying God's countless gifts, including salvation in Jesus Christ.

Yes, dancing can be vulgar and coarse, but as with David, God looks into our hearts to see what is there. Our very life should be one long song and dance for Jesus.

Dancers are the athletes of God.

-- Albert Einstein

While dancing and music can be vulgar and obscene, they can also be inspiring expressions of abiding love for God.

HAVE A HEART

Read 1 Samuel 13:1-14.

"The Lord has sought out a man after his own heart" (v. 14).

Banks McFadden knew he had just lost the broad jump. What he didn't know was that Coach Frank Howard appreciated the size of McFadden's heart and had played a trick on him.

McFadden is still regarded as the greatest all-round athlete in Clemson history. From 1936-40, he lettered three times in football, basketball, and track. In 1939, he became the first athlete in collegiate history to be named All-America in both football and basketball the same calendar year. His senior year he even pitched in one game for the baseball team. He was the first Clemson player to be inducted into the College Football Hall of Fame and was a charter member of the Clemson Athletic Hall of Fame and the South Carolina Athletic Hall of Fame. Both his basketball and his football jersey numbers have been retired.

At a track meet, a South Carolina jumper led in the broad jump. McFadden "went to the pit, measured off [his competitor's] best jump and put a handkerchief down on the ground beside the pit at that point." He then turned and trudged back up the runway.

When he hit the takeoff board, McFadden realized he wouldn't make it to the handkerchief. "That handkerchief looked like it was a mile away," he said. But he wasn't ready to give up. "I poured every ounce of myself into that take off and that jump" -- and came up short. Then to McFadden's surprise, the PA announcer declared that he had just set a new state record.

It seems that while McFadden had walked back up the runway, Howard, who was coaching track at the time, had moved the handkerchief a foot farther from the takeoff board.

Banks McFadden's heart had helped him accomplish what he couldn't manage on physical ability alone.

We all face defeat even as Banks McFadden did that weekend in Clinton, S.C. Sometimes, even though we fight with all we have, we lose. Even Clemson loses some games.

At some time, you probably have admitted you were whipped no matter how much it hurt. Always in your life, though, you have known that you would fight for some things with all your heart and never give them up: your family, your country, your friends, your core beliefs.

God should be on that list too. God seeks men and women who will never turn their back on him because they are people after God's own heart. That is, they will never betray God with their unbelief; they will never lose their childlike trust in God; they will never cease to love God with all their heart.

They are lifetime members of God's team; it's a mighty good one to be on, but it takes heart.

It's not just talent; it's heart and effort and desire.
-- Clemson tennis coach Chuck Kriese

**To be on God's team requires the heart
of a champion.**

TEARS IN HEAVEN

Read Revelation 21:1-8.

"[God] will wipe every tear from their eyes. There will be no more death or mourning or crying or pain" (v. 4).

Jeff Davis couldn't hold back the tears anymore.

Davis may well be the greatest linebacker in Clemson football history. He came to Clemson in 1978 and was a star on the 1981 national champions, recording what was then a school-record 175 tackles.

He still holds the Clemson career record for caused fumbles and recovered fumbles, and his 24 tackles against North Carolina in 1980 is still the school record for tackles in an ACC game. His 469 career tackles are still third in school history. During the forty games he played between 1978-81, he was an amazing model of consistency with 30 games in which he recorded double digits in tackles, including 22 of his last 23 games. He racked up 14 tackles in the Orange-Bowl win over Nebraska that clinched the national championship.

In 1981, he was named MVP of the ACC, just the third defensive player in league history to be so honored. He was All-America and went on to a six-year NFL career.

So what could make Davis say, with tears rolling down his face, "It is hard to believe a linebacker can get soft"? What set the tears flowing was the announcement in May 2007 that he would be among the twelve players inducted into the College Football

Hall of Fame in December. He was just the third Clemson player in history – the others are Terry Kinard and Banks McFadden – to be enshrined in the hall.

Jeff Davis fought those tears, but he finally couldn't help but choke up.

When your parents died. When a friend told you she was divorcing. When you broke your collarbone. When you watch a sad movie.

You cry. Crying is as much a part of life as are breathing and eating. Usually our tears are brought on by pain, disappointment, or sorrow.

But what about when your child was born? When you receive an honor as Jeff Davis did? When you discovered Jesus Christ? Those times elicit tears too; we cry at the times of our greatest, most overwhelming joy.

Thus, while there will be tears in Heaven, they will only be tears of sheer, unmitigated, undiluted joy. The greatest joy possible, a joy beyond our imagining, must occur when we finally see Christ. If we shed tears when Clemson wins a football game, can we really believe that we will stand dry-eyed and calm in the presence of Jesus?

What we will not shed in Heaven are tears of sorrow and pain.

If I cry, it means I'm too weak to compete in this sport. That's bull.
-- NASCAR driver Shawna Robinson

Tears in Heaven will be like everything else there:
a part of the joy we will experience.

FACING THE MUSIC

Read Psalm 98.

"Sing to the Lord a new song, for he has done marvelous things" (v. 1).

One of the great college hymns." So has the Clemson Alma Mater been described. It arose from a moment of humiliation and embarrassment.

In 1918, during the final months of World War I, some Clemson cadets were on maneuvers with other ROTC officers in Plattsburg, New York. During an assembly, each group was invited to sing its alma mater. Students from other schools proudly and loudly belted forth their songs while the Clemson students awaited their turn and fidgeted. Their discomfort sprang from a simple source: Clemson didn't have an alma mater. Instead of singing, they fired up the place with some of the cheers used during football games.

One student, Albert C. Corcoran, went back to Clemson and composed words appropriate for an alma mater. In 1919, the student newspaper published them. One rather glaring problem still remained, though: There was no music.

The school solved that problem by adopting the tune of Cornell's Alma Mater, "Above Cayuga's Waters." The glee club first performed the Clemson Alma Mater on Feb. 17, 1919, during chapel services.

In 1947, a contest was held to find an original tune. An architecture student and member of the glee club, Robert E. Farmer of

Anderson, won the contest. He could neither read nor write music, so he sang the melody to a musician friend, who wrote it down. Farmer's tune had some "inherent flaws in melody and harmony," and Hugh McGarity, the director of the glee club and the band, altered it. The new official Clemson Alma Mater was sung for the first time at the 1950 graduation exercises. A new band arrangement emerged in the 1970s and is the one still used today.

Maybe you can't carry a tune in the proverbial bucket, so that when the Clemson Tiger Marching Band plays the Alma Mater, you sort of hum along and move your lips a little. Or perhaps you do know your way around a guitar or a keyboard and can croon on karaoke night quite nicely.

Unless you're a professional musician, how well you play or sing really doesn't matter. What counts is that you have music in your heart and sometimes you have to turn it loose.

Worshipping God has always included music in some form. That same reverence you show by your singing the Alma Mater and that enthusiasm you show by your cheer when the music ends should be a part of the joy you have in your personal worship of God.

When you consider that God loves you, he always will, and he has arranged through Jesus for you to spend eternity with him, how can that song God put in your heart not burst forth?

I like it because it plays old music.
-- Pitcher Tug McGraw on his '54 Buick

You call it music; others may call it noise;
God calls it praise.

IN SO MANY WORDS

Read Matthew 12:33-37.

*"For out of the overflow of the heart the mouth speaks.
The good man brings good things out of the good stored
up in him, and the evil man brings evil things out of the
evil stored up in him" (vv. 34b-35).*

When the baseball Tigers made the 1958 NCAA postseason tournament, their games were broadcast live on the radio – thanks to the South Carolina Gamecock announcer.

Bob Fulton was the voice of the Gamecocks for 43 years. Back in 1958, college baseball didn't merit radio or television broadcasts. But when first-year coach Bill Wilhelm led the Tigers to the tournament, Fulton, of all people, thought the Tigers deserved radio coverage. He convinced the management of Columbia radio station WCOS that it was a good idea, and Clemson fans were totally delighted, no matter who was getting the word out.

What Fulton did wasn't that uncommon then. "I used to do both USC and Clemson games in the ACC basketball tournament," he recalled. That crossover announcing doesn't mean that the rivalry wasn't as spirited as it is now. It was "just as heated in 1958," Fulton said, "but no one seemed to mind my doing the games. I never got one letter of complaint."

At what was then the equivalent of today's super regional, the Tigers had to beat Florida twice to get to the College World Series. They won the first game in a 15-14 thriller when Bailey Hendley

TIGERS

singled Larry Wilson home in the bottom of the ninth. Harold Stowe then threw a four-hitter for a 3-1 win, and it was on to Omaha.

Except that Fulton wasn't really there; he never left the WCOS studio. "I set it up with Western Union for them to feed me a ticker of each pitch and each play," he remembered. "Then I filled in the color and descriptions, and an engineer provided the crowd nose. It worked pretty well."

These days, everybody's got something to say and likely as not a place to say it. Talk radio, 24-hour sports and news TV channels, *Oprah*, *The View*. Talk has really become cheap.

But words still have power, and that includes not just those of the talking heads, hucksters, and pundits on television, but ours also. Our words are perhaps the most powerful force we possess for good or for bad. The words we speak today can belittle, wound, humiliate, and destroy. They can also inspire, heal, protect, and create. Our words both shape and define us. They also reveal to the world the depth of our faith.

We should never make the mistake of underestimating the power of the spoken word. After all, speaking the Word was the only means Jesus had to get his message across – and look what he managed to do.

We must always watch what we say, because others sure will.

My daddy always taught me these words: care and share.
– Tiger Woods

Choose your words carefully; they are the most powerful force you have for good or for bad.

PAIN RELIEF

Read 2 Corinthians 1:3-7.

*"Just as the sufferings of Christ flow over into our lives,
so also through Christ our comfort overflows" (v. 5).*

In one devastating moment, all of Perry Tuttle's hopes, dreams, and plans were swept away. It was the best thing that ever happened to him.

Tuttle is one of Clemson's greatest wide receivers. He played for the Tigers from 1978-81 and was a first-team All-America in 1981. He set school records for receptions and yards and is still second all-time in receiving yards and touchdown receptions.

Three years into Tuttle's pro career, "the dream could not have been sweeter," he said. He had just bought a house and "was basking in the Florida sunshine."

But as he prepared for a weekend game, the head coach called him into his office and said five words: "We don't need you anymore." Tuttle was devastated, and the coach left him a moment so he could gather his emotions. Tuttle fled without seeing him again, going home "to wallow in my self pity."

His best friend and teammate at Clemson, Jeff Davis, came over after practice, sharing Tuttle's disbelief that he had been cut. Davis asked Tuttle if he could pray for him, and Tuttle "hesitantly" agreed. After his friend left, Tuttle said, "I gathered my broken spirit and my broken dreams and casually went to the God who I had heard my Mom pray to all my life, and the one who Jeff had

TIGERS

just prayed to, and I asked him to come into my life."

The worst day of Perry Tuttle's life was suddenly transformed by the presence of Jesus into the best day of his life. And even as he rejoiced in his salvation, his phone rang. Coach Dan Henning of the Atlanta Falcons was calling. Tuttle had left the team offices so quickly he hadn't heard all the details: He hadn't been cut; he had been traded.

Since you live on earth and not in heaven, pain will bludgeon you at some time in your life. Whether it's a car wreck that left you shattered, the end of a relationship that left you battered, or a loved one's death that left you tattered – devastating pain will find you.

While God's word teaches that you will reap what you sow, life also teaches that pain and hardship are not necessarily the result of personal failure. Pain in fact can be one of the tools God uses to mold your character and change your life.

What are you to do when you are hit full-speed as Perry Tuttle was by the awful pain that seems to choke the very will to live out of you? Where is your consolation, your comfort, and your help?

Exactly where Tuttle found it: In almighty God, whose love will never fail. When life knocks you to your knees, you're closer to God than ever before.

The Lord allowed my whole world, which was football, to be taken from me for a few hours – long enough to draw me to Him.
-- Perry Tuttle

**When life hits you with pain, you can always turn
to God for comfort, consolation, and hope.**

JUGGERNAUT

Read Revelation 20.

"Fire came down from heaven and devoured them. And the devil, who deceived them, was thrown into the lake of burning sulfur, where the beast and the false prophet had been thrown" (vv. 9b-10a).

White meat." So declared philosopher-sage-coach Frank Howard about the Clemson-Virginia series.

From 1955 through 1989, white meat is what the Virginia Cavaliers were for the Clemson football team: a delicacy served up for the Tigers to devour. Younger Clemson fans may well see the Virginia rivalry today as one of the most hotly contested in the ACC. After all, from 1990 through 2008, the Tigers went 7-8-1 against the Cavs. What those with short memories may not recall, however, is that prior to Virginia's 20-7 win in 1990, Clemson had beaten the Cavaliers an incredible 29 times in a row, establishing a dynasty that is the fourth longest in NCAA football history. Only Notre Dame over Navy (43 years), Nebraska over Kansas (36 years), and Oklahoma over Kansas State (32 years) were longer.

Once as Howard strolled across the UVA stadium the day before a game, a Virginia fan called out, "Frank, we're going to beat you tomorrow." The ever-ready Howard replied, "Yeah, that's what yo' granddaddy said, too."

Howard, Hootie Ingram, Red Parker, Charley Pell, and Danny Ford never lost to Virginia. The rumor mill insisted that Ford hated the Virginia game more than any other because he didn't want to be the one to snap the streak, considering it to be the ultimate example of a game in which his team had everything to lose and nothing to gain.

Only eight of the 29 wins were decided by seven points or fewer. The biggest romp of all was the 55-0 slaughter of 1984. For 29 years, the Clemson Tigers were a juggernaut the Virginia Cavaliers couldn't stop.

Maybe your experience with a juggernaut involved a high-school game against a team full of major college prospects, a league tennis match against a former college player, or your presentation for the project you knew didn't stand a chance. Whatever it was, you've been slam-dunked before.

Being part of a juggernaut is certainly more fun than being in the way of one. Just ask the many Virginia players who never beat Clemson. Or consider the forces of evil aligned against God. At least the Cavaliers every year had some hope, however slim, that they might win. No such hope exists for those who oppose God.

That's because their fate is already spelled out in detail. It's in the book; we all know how the story ends. God's enemies may talk big and bluster now, but they will be trounced in the most decisive defeat of all time.

You sure want to be on the winning side in that one.

I'd never been to a mercy killing before.
  -- New Orleans Basketball Coach Benny Dees after a 101-76 loss

The most lopsided victory in all of history is a sure thing: God's ultimate triumph over evil.

COMEBACK KIDS

Read Acts 9:1-22.

"All those who heard him were astonished and asked, 'Isn't he the man who raised havoc in Jerusalem among those who call on this name?'" (v. 21)

In one of the greatest seasons ever, the Clemson men's basketball team pulled off the greatest last-half comeback in school history.

The Tigers of 2007-08 went 24-10 and advanced to the finals of the ACC Tournament and to the NCAA Tournament. On March 2 against Maryland, though, the team looked awful for much of the game. With 11:21 remaining, the Terps led 59-39 and seemed poised to hand the Tigers their worst loss of the season. A comeback of this proportion seemed unlikely; the biggest last-half comeback in school history was 19 points, pulled off against LaSalle in the 1990 NCAA Tournament.

But senior forward James Mays poured in 16 of his season-high 20 points in the last half to ignite a furious rally. Clemson got within seven before Maryland stretched the margin back to 13 with 6:37 to go. Mays then discarded the bandage on his injured left hand and produced a tip-in, a 3-point play, and a dunk that roared the Tigers to 68-64 with 2:49 left. With the margin only two points, Mays stole a pass and drove the court for the tying dunk with 45 seconds left.

Maryland shot, and Sam Perry grabbed the rebound with 18 seconds left. After a time out, guard K.C. Rivers found freshman guard Terrence Oglesby open, and he calmly nailed a trey for the stunning 73-70 win.

"It wasn't just me. It wasn't just one play," Oglesby said. "This team never quit."

After Oglesby's shot, the team gathered at the Clemson bench in jubilation and celebration while a dismayed and silent Maryland crowd looked on, still not believing the comeback Clemson had managed.

Life will have its setbacks whether they result from personal failures or from forces and people beyond your control. Being a Christian and a faithful follower of Jesus Christ doesn't insulate you from getting into deep trouble. Maybe financial problems suffocated you. A serious illness put you on the sidelines. Or your family was hit with a great tragedy. Life is a series of victories and defeats. Winning isn't about avoiding defeat; it's about getting back up to compete again. It's about making a comeback of your own.

When you avail yourself of God's grace and God's power, your comeback is always greater than your setback. You are never too far behind, and it's never too late in life's game for Jesus to lead you to victory, to turn trouble into triumph. As it was with the Clemson Tigers against Maryland and with Paul, it's not how you start that counts; it's how you finish.

Turn a setback into a comeback.

-- *Football coach Billy Brewer*

In life, victory is truly a matter of how you finish and whether you finish with Jesus at your side.

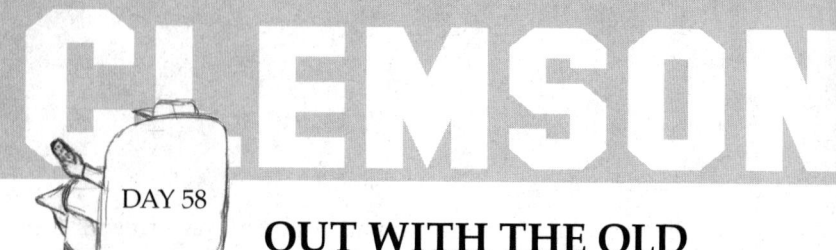

OUT WITH THE OLD

Read Hebrews 8:3-13.

"The ministry Jesus has received is as superior to theirs as the covenant of which he is mediator is superior to the old one, and it is founded on better promises" (v. 6).

Coach John Heisman's old way of doing things will never return to supplant the modern game or the way college football coaches handle their players today.

The man after whom college football's most prestigious award is named coached at Clemson from 1900-03 "and turned Clemson from virtually an unknown college to a southern powerhouse." His record was 19-3-2, and his .833 winning percentage remains the best in Tiger history.

Successful though he was, Heisman was definitely an old-time coach with some rather antiquated and eccentric ways of approaching training and the games. For instance, his players couldn't eat pork or pastry, nor were they allowed soap or hot water in the shower. He decreed that a football coach "should be masterful and commanding, even dictatorial" with "no time to say 'please' or 'mister.' At times he must be severe, arbitrary and little short of a czar." On the players' lockers, Heisman posted a series of "don'ts" that included "don't forget to stiff-arm," "don't forget your signals," "don't cuss," and – perhaps most extraneously – "don't lose the game."

Heisman also coached the game itself with a strict set of rules

TIGERS

that allowed for no imagination or improvisation and that demonstrate that his football really was from a bygone era: No end runs on first or second downs and never two end runs in succession; no passes inside your own 30 yard line with third down the best down to pass on; punts on first down if the ball is close to your own goal; and "when in doubt, punt anyway, anywhere."

Time and innovation have passed John Heisman's brand of football and coaching by.

Your car's running fine, but the miles are adding up. Your TV's still delivering a sharp picture, but those HDTV's are really something. Same with the newer, faster computers. And how about those lawn mowers that turn on a dime?

Out with the old, in with the new — we're always looking for the newest thing on the market. In our faith life, that means the new covenant God gave us through Jesus Christ. An old covenant did exist, one based on the law God handed down to the Hebrew people. But God used this old covenant as the basis to go one better and establish a covenant available to the whole world.

This new way is a covenant of grace between God and anyone who lives a life of faith in Jesus. Don't get caught waiting for a newer, improved covenant, though; the promises God gave us through Jesus couldn't get any better.

The old ballplayer cared about the name on the front [of the jersey]. The new ballplayer cares about the name on the back.
— Former major leaguer Steve Garvey

**No matter how old it is,
it just doesn't get any better
than God's new covenant through Jesus Christ.**

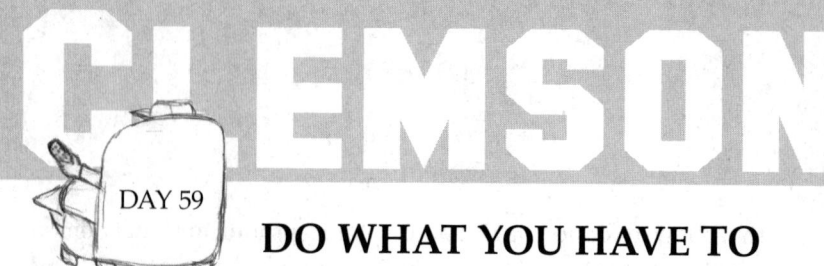

DO WHAT YOU HAVE TO

Read 2 Samuel 12:1-15a.

"The Lord sent Nathan to David" (v. 1).

What has been described as "the most exciting 25 seconds in college football from a color and pageantry standpoint" started out from necessity. The Tigers had to do it.

The first 20,000 seats in Clemson Memorial Stadium were ready for the 1942 season. The shortest route into the stadium for the players was a walk down Williamson Road from Fike Field House's dressing room to a gate at the top of the hill behind the east end zone. The west end zone had no dressing rooms, "only a big clock where the hands turned, and a scoreboard, which was operated by hand."

So the team would make that walk and quietly jog down the hill and line up for its warm-up exercises. The players went down the hill because they had to.

The team members started rubbing Howard's Rock prior to running down the hill on Sept. 23, 1967. After the construction of the dressing rooms in the west end zone, Coach Hootie Ingram decided prior to the 1970 season that the team should enter the most convenient way. So in 1970, '71, and part of '72, the Tigers didn't run down the hill. Their record at home was a lousy 6-9. The players decided to come down the hill prior to the South Carolina game in 1972; they won 7-6.

TIGERS

Ever since then, the Tigers have come down the hill by boarding two buses and riding around behind the north stands to the east end zone. Only now, when the team comes down the hill, the cannon booms, the tiger paw flag makes its run, the band strikes up "Tiger Rag," and the frenzy starts in earnest.

And it all started because of something the football team had to do.

You've also had to do some things in your life, including many you didn't want to. Maybe when you put your daughter on severe restriction, broke the news of a death in the family, fired a friend, or underwent surgery. You plowed again because you knew it was for the best or you had no choice.

Nathan surely didn't want to confront King David and tell him what a miserable reprobate he'd been, but the prophet had no choice: Obedience to God overrode all other factors. Of all that God asks of us in the living of a godly life, obedience is perhaps the most difficult. After all, our history of disobedience stretches all the way back to the Garden of Eden. The problem is that God expects obedience not only when his wishes match our own but also when they don't.

Obedience to God is a way of life, not a matter of convenience.

Coaching is making men do what they don't want, so they can become what they want to be.
-- Tom Landry

You can never foresee what God will demand
of you, but obedience requires being ready
to do whatever God asks.

DAY 60

DOWNRIGHT CRAZY

Read Luke 13:31-35.

"Some Pharisees came to Jesus and said to him, 'Leave this place and go somewhere else. Herod wants to kill you.' He replied, 'Go tell that fox . . . I must keep going today and tomorrow and the next day'" (vv. 31-33).

Clemson football coach Danny Ford couldn't believe the crazy thing he saw his team doing. With the clock ticking away the last few seconds and no time-outs left, they were huddling up.

The 1987 Tigers were 2-0 and ranked in the top ten when they welcomed the Georgia Bulldogs into Death Valley on Sept. 19. Georgia scored with 8:59 left in the game to take a 20-16 lead and then forced a punt. But John Johnson downed punter Rusty Seyle's high kick at the Georgia one, and on second down, James Lott and Gene Beasley sacked the Bulldog quarterback for a safety. 20-18. After the free kick, the Tigers then marched to the Georgia five, and that's when things turned from thrilling to slightly crazy.

Clemson had no way to stop the clock, which relentlessly and steadfastly ticked under 20 seconds and kept going. Kicker David Treadwell and holder Greg Bailey were ready – while the rest of the unit huddled up off to the side. "I couldn't believe it when our guys went out and huddled up," Ford said. "I could just see us . . . letting the clock run down and not get[ting] the kick off. We practice running on the field without a huddle in those situations, but we must not have practiced it too well last week."

While Ford, his staff, the Tiger players on the sideline, and the nail-biting fans in the stands watched helplessly and anxiously, the offense quite deliberately broke the huddle and settled into position as the clock ticked down to single digits. With two seconds left, Treadwell's kick was true. Clemson had a 21-20 win.

In retrospect, the crazy huddle was quite shrewd; Georgia didn't even have enough time left to attempt a desperate pass or a long field goal.

What some see as crazy often is shrewd instead. Like the time you went into business for yourself or when you decided to go back to school. Maybe it was when you fixed up that old house. Or when you bought that new company's stock.

You know a good thing when you see it but are also shrewd enough to spot something that's downright crazy. Jesus was that way too. He knew that entering Jerusalem was in complete defiance of all apparent reason and logic since a whole bunch of folks who wanted to kill him were waiting for him there. He would be on their turf, not his.

Nevertheless, he went because he also knew that when the great drama had played out he would defeat not only his personal enemies but the most fearsome enemy of all: death itself.

It was, after all, a shrewd move that accomplished his mission and provided the way to your salvation.

Football is easy if you're crazy.

-- Bo Jackson

It's so good it sounds crazy -- but it's not: through faith in Jesus, you can have eternal life with God.

ROCK SOLID

Read Luke 6:46-49.

"I will show you what he is like who comes to me and hears my words and puts them into practice. He is like a man building a house, who dug down deep and laid the foundation on rock" (vv. 47-48).

It was the foundation for Clemson's athletic success and "was ahead of its time in almost every respect." It was and is IPTAY.

After the one-win season of 1931, Clemson football coach Jess Neely wistfully observed, "If we could just find $10,000 a year for the athletic program, we could get somewhere." Neely was speaking very practically because the cupboard was bare in Clemson. The coaches had to sew torn sweatshirts, pick up rocks from athletic fields, repair shoulder pads, work at the canteen counter, and sell and take up tickets.

A plan was in the works, though, hatched in the "wild brain" of Dr. Rupert Fike, a 1908 Clemson graduate who was a cancer specialist. Fike told Neely, "Maybe we can find enough people with ten bucks to do the trick." And then he uttered a strange acronym that has since become as much a part of Clemson as The Paw: IPTAY. "IPTAY will do it," he said. "We can find a thousand Clemson men who will give ten dollars every year."

IPTAY is a soaring success now, but it wasn't "born with a silver spoon in its mouth." Only 185 people "became disciples of the cause during its first year." But Fike and some of his fellow believers took the story of IPTAY across the state, enlisting donors one at a time, until it became "the heart, the life's blood, the muscle of the Clemson athletic program." More than anything else, IPTAY was the foundation upon which was built the magnificent program that is Clemson athletics today.

Like Clemson's entire athletics program, your life is an ongoing project, a work in progress. As with any complex construction job, if your life is to be stable, it must have a solid foundation, which holds everything up and keeps everything together.

R. Alan Culpepper said in *The New Interpreter's Bible*, "We do not choose whether we will face severe storms in life; we only get to choose the foundation on which we will stand." In other words, tough times are inevitable. If your foundation isn't rock-solid, you will have nothing on which to stand as those storms buffet you, nothing to keep your life from flying apart into a cycle of disappointment and destruction.

But when the foundation is solid and sure, you can take the blows, stand strong, recover, and live with joy and hope. Only one foundation is sure and foolproof: Jesus Christ. Everything else you build upon will fail you.

When I was younger, I thought that the key to success was just hard work. But the real foundation is faith.
-- Former NFL player Howard Twilley

In the building of your life, you must start with a foundation in Jesus Christ, or the first trouble that shows up will knock you down.

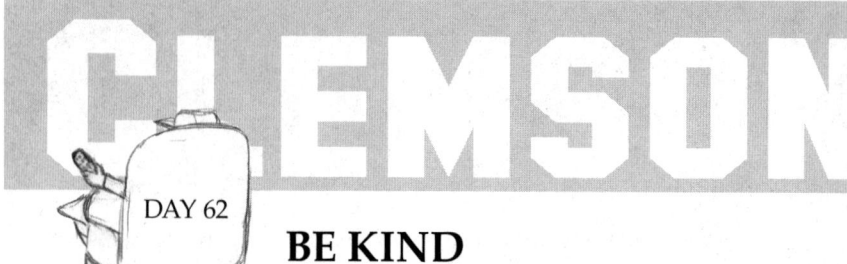

DAY 62

BE KIND

Read Ephesians 4:17-32.

*"Be kind and compassionate to one another, forgiving each
other, just as in Christ God forgave you" (v. 32).*

A simple act of kindness led to the hiring of a Clemson legend.

Fred Hoover worked for the Clemson Athletic Department as
a trainer from 1958 until his retirement after the 1998 season, a
string of 40 straight football seasons. When he retired, he had
worked on the sidelines for more than 440 straight games. He
coordinated the training room needs of more than 900 Clemson
football players and worked under seven different head coaches.
He ran down the hill with the Clemson football team more than
200 times.

"Fred Hoover is simply an establishment," said then-head
coach Tommy West when Hoover announced his retirement. He's
"respected everywhere in this country," athletics director Bobby
Robinson said. Frank Howard described him as "one of the most
recognized people ever in Clemson athletics." In 1982, he was
inducted into the Clemson Athletic Hall of Fame.

And he got the job in the first place back in 1958 because he was
kind. Howard was in Tallahassee for a coaching clinic. He had a
new set of false teeth that, as he explained it, "had a high spot
on them and I was sitting there with some sandpaper, trying to
smooth it down." The word was out that Howard was looking for
a trainer, and Hoover approached him about the job. They talked

and Hoover left but then returned a few minutes later with an emery board. He told Howard it would do a better job than sandpaper on his false teeth and urged the coach to try it. It worked.

"I figured that anybody who was that considerate must be a pretty good fella," Howard said. "So I told him that he had the job if he wanted it." Hoover did, and the makings of a Clemson legend had begun.

All because of a simple act of kindness.

We may all talk about kindness, but moving beyond the talk to actually demonstrating kindness to others is so exceptional in our world that we take notice of it. The person who finds a wallet with cash in it and returns it to the owner merits a spot on the evening news. So does the millionaire who gives a big chunk of change to a hospital or a charity. And Frank Howard was so impressed with Fred Hoover's kindness in procuring and then offering him an emery board that he offered him a job on the spot.

Practicing kindness is difficult because it requires that we move beyond our own selves to the recognition of the needs of others; a kind person places others first. In an impersonal world, a kind person goes to the time and the trouble to establish personal contact – just as Jesus did and just as God did when he sent Jesus to us.

You can motivate players better with kind words than with a whip.
– Former coach Bud Wilkinson

**Practicing kindness is hard
because it requires us to place others first,
exactly the way Jesus lived among us.**

DAY 63

THE MOTHER LODE

Read John 19:25-30.

"Near the cross of Jesus stood his mother" (v. 25).

Among the most decorated student-athletes in Clemson history, basketball guard Cliff Hammonds was also a man of character. He inherited it from his mama.

Hammonds was the 2007-08 IPTAY Athlete of the Year and third-team All-ACC, which speaks of his athletic ability. But he was also such an inspiration in the classroom that the School of Architecture presented him with an award created just for him in honor of his "quiet leadership, discipline, and collegiality."

Architecture professor Lynn Craig said of the award, "We've never done anything like this before, but we've never seen anyone quite like Cliff." Hammonds graduated in 2008, the first Clemson scholarshipped basketball player ever to earn an architecture degree.

Nowhere was his leadership, discipline, and character demonstrated more than in January 2007 when he led the Tigers to a 68-66 win over FSU, scoring the winning basket with just 2.3 seconds left.

He played so hard that he was totally dehydrated after the game, helped off the court by his teammates. He needed multiple IVs in the locker room. While he was in the training room, his mother came in to check on him. She stood next to him while he lay on the training table, "rubbing his legs and singing a gospel hymn, trying to help him get through the discomfort." She stayed with her son until he was strong enough to walk out.

As Tim Bourret, Clemson's Sports Information Director, put it, "I will always remember that moment because it showed me why Cliff Hammonds was a person of high character. He came by it naturally."

Mamas often do things like that: standing by or sacrificing personal happiness for their children's sake. No mother in history, though, has faced a challenge to match that of Mary, whom God chose to be the mother of Jesus. Like mamas and their children throughout time, Mary experienced both joy and perplexity in her relationship with her son.

To the end, though, Mary stood by her boy. She followed him all the way to his execution, an act of love and bravery since Jesus was condemned as an enemy of the Roman Empire.

But just as mothers like Mary and Cliff Hammonds' mom -- and perhaps yours -- would apparently do anything for their children, so will God do anything out of love for his children. After all, that was God on the cross at the foot of which Mary stood, and he was dying for you, one of his children.

I did such a good job one time on selling Clemson to this boy's mama that she came to Clemson and he went to South Carolina.
— Frank Howard

Mamas often sacrifice for their children,
but God, too, will do anything out of love
for his children, including dying on a cross.

DAY 64

CHANGELESS

Read Hebrews 13:5-16.

"Jesus Christ is the same yesterday and today and forever" (v. 8).

Things have sure changed.

When football began at Clemson, the students raised the money to fund the team through the Football Aid Society, which netted $372.50 with its first fund drive. The players picked their own coach, an engineering professor, who in turn chose the school colors of purple and gold and the school mascot.

The players didn't wear helmets and protected themselves by letting their hair grow long. A nose guard was about the only protection they had unless they provided shoulder pads or hip pads themselves. The ball they used was the shape of a watermelon, too big to hold in a hand and pass.

Things were quite different on the field too. A player might hide the ball under his jersey. Spectators often got in the players' way by rushing onto the field. Players dragged tackled ball carriers forward. Teams decided upon the length of games once they showed up to play. Linemen held hands and jumped to either side just before a play began. When dusk began to fall, spectators' automobiles were sometimes used to light up the field.

This was the wild and wooly game of college football in its early days, the 1890s and the turn of the century. Largely unregulated and unsophisticated, it was a game we would scarcely recognize today.

Thank goodness, we might well say. Given the symmetry, the excitement, the passion, and the sheer spectacle that surround today's college game, few, if any, Clemson fans would long for the days when handles were sewn into uniforms to make ball carriers easier to toss.

Like everything else, football has changed. Computers and CDs, cell phones and George Foreman grills, iPods and IMAX theaters – they and much that is common in your life now may not have even been around when you were 16. Think about how style, cars, communications, and tax laws constantly change.

Don't be too harsh on the world, though, because you've changed also. You've aged, gained or lost weight, gotten married, changed jobs, or relocated.

Have you ever found yourself bewildered by the rapid pace of change, casting about for something to hold on to that will always be the same, that you can use as an anchor for your life? Is there anything like that?

Sadly, the answer's no. All the things of this world change.

On the other hand, there's Jesus, who is the same today, the same forever, always dependable, always loving you. You can grab hold of Jesus and never let go.

I'm not too proud to change. I like to win too much.

-- Bobby Bowden

**In our ever-changing and bewildering world,
Jesus is the same forever;
his love for you will never change.**

DAY 65

JUST PERFECT

Read Matthew 5:43-48.

"Be perfect, therefore, as your heavenly Father is perfect"
(v. 48).

To be able to say I never lost to South Carolina, that's something I can take for the rest of my life. That's something nobody can take away from me."

Prior to the 2005 game against South Carolina, senior Tiger cornerback Tye Hill thus expressed the sentiments of a rare breed of Cats: those who never lost a football game to the Gamecocks. Perfection is rare indeed, and only four Clemson classes since 1941 have been perfect against South Carolina: the classes of 1983, 1991, 2000, and Hill's 2005 team.

That 2005 win will forever be known as the game of "First and 35." When USC kicked a field goal early in the fourth quarter to lead 9-6, the Gamecocks appeared to be in command. Their defense had been so dominating that Coach Tommy Bowden considered benching four-year starting quarterback Charlie Whitehurst. Instead, Bowden turned to Whitehurst and said, "Go to work."

He almost didn't get a chance as penalties on consecutive plays left the Tigers facing the now-famous first and 35 at their own 22 with about nine minutes left to play. Almost before anybody realized what was happening, Clemson scored. Whitehurst hit passes for 9, 14, and 28 yards. James Davis then ran for 23, 2, and

2 yards, the latter run leaving him standing in the end zone with the game's only touchdown.

Clemson had a 13-9 win, and the seniors of 2005 were perfect.

Nobody's always perfect; even those Clemson seniors who were perfect against USC lost other games. The plain truth is we all make mistakes every day. We botch our personal relationships; at work we seek competence, not perfection. To insist upon personal or professional perfection in our lives is to establish an impossibly high standard that eventually destroys us physically, emotionally, and mentally.

Yet that is exactly the standard God sets for us. Our love is to be perfect, never ceasing, never failing, never qualified – just the way God loves us. And Jesus didn't limit his command to only preachers and goody-two-shoes types. All of his disciples are to be perfect as they navigate their way through the world's ambiguous definition and understanding of love.

But that's impossible! Well, not necessarily if to love perfectly is to serve God wholeheartedly and to follow Jesus with single-minded devotion. Anyhow, in his perfect love for us, God makes allowance for our imperfect love and the consequences of it in the perfection of Jesus.

Practice does not make you perfect as nobody is perfect, but it does make you better.
--Soccer coach Adrian Parrish

In his perfect love for us, God provides a way for us to escape the consequences of our imperfect love for him: Jesus.

DAY 66

TOUGH LOVE

Read Mark 10:17-22.

*"Jesus looked at him and loved him. 'One thing you lack,'
he said. 'Go, sell everything you have and give to the poor,
and you will have treasure in heaven. Then come, follow
me.' At this the man's face fell. He went away sad, because
he had great wealth" (vv. 21-22).*

Don't come home. Find a job."

As a sophomore in 1978, Reggie Herring called his father to tell
him he had quit the FSU football team. That's when he got the
six-word lesson in tough love that changed his life. He led FSU in
tackles the next three seasons and became a college coach.

When Tommy Bowden brought Herring to Clemson in 1993 as
linebackers coach and eventually defensive coordinator, Herring
brought his own brand of tough love with him. He was known
to scream so loud and so often at his players that he periodically
went hoarse. "It's kind of like hard love," said linebacker Chad
Carson, a three-time Academic All-America whom Herring once
picked up, threw over to the offensive team, and told not to come
back. "He is trying to make you better."

When Will Merritt, a second-team All-ACC guard in 2001, made
a mistake on the scout team, Herring threatened to rip his head
off, kick it into a moat, and make Merritt swim around until he
found it. Later, Herring sort of apologized, saying, "Will, I really
wouldn't make you go look for your head."

And Herring's reaction was the stuff of legend the day a freshman reported to practice wearing jewelry.

Herring's Clemson defenses were consistently among the nation's best, especially in 2000 when the Tigers were 9-3 and the defense was ranked 18th in the country against the rush and 23rd in scoring defense. Bowden said, "Our defense reflects Reggie's personality and playing style. That's good, because [defense] is played with great emotion and great intensity."

And in Reggie Herring's case with tough love.

Expect your children to abide by your rules? The immediate reward you receive may be an intense and loud "I hate you," a flounce, and a slammed door. So why do it? Because you're the parent; you love your children, and you want them to become responsible adults. It's tough love.

Jesus also hands out tough love as the story of the young man illustrates. Jesus broke his heart, but the failure was in the young man, who despite his asseverations of devotion, loved his wealth more than he did Jesus.

Jesus is tough on us, too, in that he expects us to follow him no matter what it costs us. A well-executed flounce won't change anything either. As a parent does for his willful children, Jesus knows what is best for us. We'll appreciate that tough love with all our heart and soul on that glorious day when Jesus welcomes us to the place he has prepared for us.

The sterner the discipline, the greater the devotion.
— Basketball coach Pete Carill

**Jesus expects us to do what he has told us to do —
but it's because he loves us and wants the best
for us in life and through eternity.**

DAY 67

NO TURNING BACK

Read Colossians 3:5-17.

"You have taken off your old self with its practices and have put on the new self" (vv. 9-10).

When legendary men's tennis coach Chuck Kriese decided to retire from Clemson after 33 years, he made sure there was no turning back. He took a job on the other side of the world.

In November 2007, Kriese informed athletics director Terry Don Phillips that the 2008 season would be his last. Kriese is the winningest coach in ACC tennis history with eleven ACC championships. Three times he was the national coach of the year; forty-four of his Tiger players went on to professional careers and twenty-six became college coaches.

Kriese always insisted that changes in NCAA rules hurt the Clemson program more than others. He felt the Tigers were particularly hurt by the limits on practice times and the number of matches. "What success we had, we got by outworking other teams," he said. "We were able to bridge the gap between ourselves and some higher profile schools with late bloom[ing] athletes whose hunger and work ethic was superior."

When he announced his resignation, Kriese intended to continue his summer camps and spend time working with a handful of juniors and pros. He said his wife and he "basically just prayed God would close doors where he didn't want us to go and open them where he did." One totally unexpected door kept opening wider: technical director for Southeast Asia tennis. That required a move to Bangkok, Thailand.

Perhaps appreciating the enormity of such a complete break with his past, Kriese got cold feet about moving to Thailand and considered asking Clemson for a contract extension. Ultimately, though, he said, "There was just a peace in our hearts about going." Even if it meant no turning back.

Courageous pioneers seeking a better life spread out across unfamiliar territory and in the process conquered the American wilderness. That wanderlust seems part of our national character now, and you probably inherited it. A new job, a new home, better schools for the kids -- you'll load up a U-Haul truck or the back of a pickup and head out to a new place for any number of reasons. You leave the old behind and embrace the new, knowing you can never turn back -- and not wanting to.

An encounter with Jesus Christ has a similar effect on a person's life. You leave behind the old ways; new habits beckon. You move on to a different, new, and even unfamiliar you with no desire to ever again be what you were before.

Jesus never gives you the option of turning back, so with your eyes and your heart fixed on the road ahead, you set out for bigger, better, and more glorious days.

Don't live on the fading memories of your forefathers. Go out and make your own records, and leave some memories for others to live by.
-- Legendary Vanderbilt Coach Dan McGugin

An encounter with Jesus Christ sets a life on a road to glory from which there is no turning back.

DAY 68

BLIND JUSTICE

Read Micah 6:6-8.

"He has showed you, O man, what is good. And what does the Lord require of you? To act justly and to love mercy and to walk humbly with your God" (v. 8).

The football Tigers were flat-out robbed by the officials in the 1985 Maryland game – not once but twice.

It's been called "one of the most bitter and frustrating losses of the Danny Ford era." A young Clemson team was 5-4 when the Terrapins rolled into town on Nov. 16. Clemson got a touchdown when Donnell Woolford blocked a punt and Perry Williams ran 30 yards for the score. A field goal from walk-on David Treadwell made it 10-0 before Maryland scored twice to lead 14-10.

Kenny Flowers scored from five yards out as the seesaw continued. Another blocked punt -- this one by Gene Beasley -- set up a touchdown for a 24-14 Tiger lead. Maryland rallied again and tied the game at 24. Clemson responded yet again; fullback Tracy Johnson capped an 80-yard drive with a five-yard run. Clemson led 31-24 with 5:33 remaining.

Then the refs took over. With only 1:18 left on the clock, Maryland sat with a third down inside the Tiger three. The play clock ticked down to zero, and the Terps had not snapped the ball. Ford screamed at the officials, but they ignored him as they had the play clock.

When Maryland snapped the ball, the quarterback threw

to his tight end, who dropped the ball. Incredibly, the officials signaled touchdown and allowed Maryland to tie the game at 31. The CBS replay "left little doubt that [the Maryland receiver] did not have proper possession of the pass." Nothing came of Ford's heated protestations. Instead, Maryland got the ball back with 44 seconds left and kicked a field goal in the closing seconds for a 34-31 win.

The Tigers were robbed.

Where's the justice when cars fly past you just as a state trooper pulls you over? When a con man swindles an elderly neighbor? When crooked politicians treat your tax dollars as their personal slush fund? When children starve?

Injustice enrages us, but anger is not enough. The establishment of justice in this world has to start with each one of us. The Lord requires it of us. For most of us, a just world is one in which everybody gets what he or she deserves.

But that is not God's way. God expects us to be just and merciful in all our dealings without consideration as to whether the other person "deserves" it. The justice we dispense should truly be blind. If that doesn't sound "fair," then pause and consider that when we stand before God, the last thing we want is what we deserve. We want mercy, not justice.

None of us wants justice from God. What we want is mercy because if we got justice, we'd all go to hell.

-- *Bobby Bowden*

God requires that we dispense justice and mercy without regards to deserts, exactly what we pray we will in turn receive from God.

CLOTHES HORSE

Read Genesis 37:1-11.

"Israel loved Joseph more than all his children, because he was the son of his old age: and he made him a coat of many colours" (v. 3) (KJV).

When the fans saw what the Clemson football team was wearing, they gasped in dismay. Then they roared in approval.

The 3-1-1 Tigers had gone two games without a win when undefeated North Carolina State charged into town on Nov. 2, 1991. They needed to shake things up, change some things. What they changed were their jerseys.

After warming up in their usual bright orange, the Tigers pulled a switch in the dressing room and stunned the home crowd by reappearing in purple jerseys for the first time in 52 years. While purple and orange are the official school colors, "the magenta hue [had] been largely forgotten amid the orange mania that [had] gripped the program and its fans for years."

The Tigers stopped wearing purple after the 1939 season when someone convinced coach Jess Neely that purple made the players too hot. Since then, the jerseys had been orange or white.

But the team's seniors had pressured equipment manager Doug Gordon to "get us something different." So in the spring he purchased the purple jerseys. After a tie with Virginia, Gordon reminded the seniors of the jerseys, and they asked Coach Ken Hatfield for permission to wear them.

TIGERS

"At first," said split end Terry Smith, "I thought, Oh, man, these are ugly. But once we put them on, it was sort of cool. And I believe the fans really liked it."

The fans really liked what they saw in the purple jerseys. Sporting their new duds, the Tigers whipped N.C. State 29-19.

Contemporary society proclaims that it's all about the clothes. Buy that new suit or dress, those new shoes, and all the sparkling accessories and you'll be a new person. The changes are only cosmetic, though; under those clothes, you're the same person. The Tigers still had to go out and play good football against N.C. State whether their jerseys were orange, white, or purple. And consider Joseph prancing about in his pretty new clothes; he was still a spoiled tattletale whose brother despised him.

Jesus never taught that we should run around half-naked or wear only second-hand clothes from the local mission. He did warn us, though, against making consumer items such as clothes a priority in our lives.

A follower of Christ seeks to emulate Jesus not through material, superficial means such as wearing special clothing like a robe and sandals. Rather, the disciple desires to match Jesus' inner beauty and serenity -- whether the clothes the Christian wears are the sables of a king or the rags of a pauper.

You can't call [golf] a sport. You don't run, jump, you don't shoot, you don't pass. All you have to do is buy some clothes that don't match.
-- Former major leaguer Steve Sax

**Where Jesus is concerned, clothes don't
make the person; faith does.**

THE HOME FIELD

Read Joshua 24:14-27.

"Choose for yourselves this day whom you will serve. . . .
But as for me and my household, we will serve the Lord"
(v. 15).

Clemson's baseball team has a real home-field advantage. It's called Doug Kingsmore Stadium.

The stadium has been the home of Tiger baseball since 1970. While it has undergone several renovations and changes through the years, it remains one of college baseball's most beautiful parks. In 2003, a *Baseball America* survey of college coaches ranked the stadium among the best facilities in the country. And that was before $5 million worth of renovations and improvements.

The renovations accentuated the park's unique beauty, which includes a hill down the leftfield line, a favorite of the students. The park also has a terrace in the outfield in place of the gravel warning track that alerts a player he is nearing the outfield wall.

The Clemson fans obviously enjoy the park; heading into the 2010 season, Clemson had been in the top 20 in attendance for sixteen straight seasons. The Tiger players have a big time there too. The numbers don't lie: When the Tigers play at home, they win. In the park's 40 years of play through the 2009 season, the Tiger winning percentage is a whopping 81 percent; it's 80 percent for ACC games, which is even more impressive.

In 2000, after Clemson swept No. 2 FSU in the park, Seminole

TIGERS

coach Mike Martin said, "If you had told me in 1992 that we'd be going to a place where we'd be 2-13 over the next eight years, I would have gone to the administration and suggested we join another conference."

There's just no place like home for Clemson's baseball Tigers.

Whether it's a condo, an apartment, a two-story mansion, a sprawling ranch house, or a country place with a wraparound porch, you know it as home. It's much more than a place to hang out for a while before you crash. You enter to find love, security, and joy. It is the place where your heart feels warmest, your laughter comes easiest, and your life is its richest. It is the center of and the reason for everything you do and everything you are.

How can a home be such a place?

If it is a home where grace is spoken before every meal, it is such a place. If it is a home where the Bible is read, studied, and discussed by the whole family gathered together, it is such a place. If it is a home that serves as a jumping-off point for the whole family to go to church, not just on Sunday morning and not just occasionally, but regularly. If it is a home where the name of God is spoken with reverence and awe and not with disrespect and indifference, it is such a place.

In other words, a house becomes a true home when God is part of the family.

Having a home away from the media glare is important to the world-class athlete.

-- Mary Lou Retton

A home is full when all the family members are present -- including God.

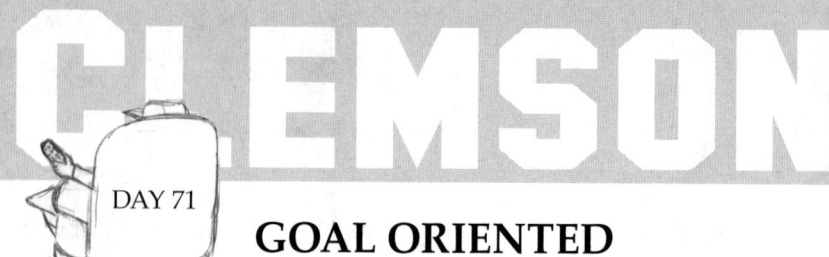

GOAL ORIENTED

Read 1 Peter 1:3-9.

"For you are receiving the goal of your faith, the salvation of your souls" (v. 9).

Y ou're 5'6" tall. You weigh 152 pounds. And you want to play football at Clemson? Yeah, right. But Carl Martin did it by trusting in God and by setting goals and working to achieve them no matter how improbable they seemed.

Martin was not a college prospect; even coaches from smaller colleges told him they "didn't need any more small, slow, football players." But he had always dreamed of playing for Clemson, so despite the disparaging assessments of his talent, he walked on in 1979.

He stuck it out, and then his life changed in 1981 when defensive backs coach Curley Hallman told his players to write down their goals for the next year. Martin's answer was vague, and another defensive back coach, Steve Hale, told him his goals needed to be more specific. So Martin wrote, "I want to make the first tackle of the opening kickoff against Tulane in the Superdome." This meant that Martin, an eighth-team strong safety, had first to make the traveling squad and then make the kickoff team.

The day before one of the preseason scrimmages, Hallman told Martin he would get his chance to show what he was capable of. The next day Martin was in on kickoffs, and he tackled Perry Tuttle. The coaches ran it again, and again Martin made the tackle.

TIGERS

The following Monday at practice, Martin found his name on the first-team kickoff squad.

The second game of the season, Tulane won the coin toss and kicked off, but when Clemson kicked off to start the second half, Martin made a solo tackle. He had achieved his seemingly impossible goal. And he also got a national championship ring in the deal.

What are your goals for your life? Have you ever thought them out? Or do you just shuffle along living for your paycheck and whatever fun you can seek out instead of pursuing some greater purpose?

Now try this one: What is the goal of your faith life? You go to church to worship God. You read the Bible and study God's word to learn about God and how God wants you to live. But what is it you hope to achieve? What is all that stuff about? For what purpose do you believe that Jesus Christ is God's son?

The answer is actually quite simple: The goal of your faith life is your salvation, and this is the only goal in life that matters. Nothing you will ever seek – even making tackles for Clemson -- is as important or as eternal as getting into Heaven and making sure that everybody you know and love will be there too one day.

Set your goal to be pleasing to God.

--- The Rev. Carl Martin

**The most important goal of your life is
to get to Heaven and to make sure those you know
and love will meet you there one day.**

IDENTITY CRISIS

Read Matthew 16:13-20.

"[Jesus] asked his disciples, 'Who do people say the Son of Man is?' They replied, 'Some say John the Baptist; others say Elijah; and still others, Jeremiah or one of the prophets'" (vv. 13-14).

The powers that be decided Clemson needed a symbol that would establish an identity around which the Tiger faithful could rally. What they came up with was The Paw.

In 1970, Clemson President Robert C. Edwards, who was such a Clemson enthusiast that even as the school president he once hitchhiked to a game rather than miss it, decided "to upgrade the image of the university." That included the creation of a unique logo that would not replace the tiger but would complement it.

A Greenville advertising company came up with the idea of using a tiger paw. To ensure accuracy, the company wrote the Museum of Natural History in Chicago and asked for a plaster of Paris imprint of an actual tiger's paw. Tilted about ten degrees to the right, this imprint was the basis for The Paw (unlike Penn State's anatomically incorrect paw, which has five toes). As Wright Bryan, the university's vice president for development, said on a whirlwind tour to introduce The Paw across the state, "There needs to be some symbol which keeps the whole thing together."

Not everyone was enthusiastic about The Paw at first. Even Coach Frank Howard didn't think much of it. But Clemson fans

TIGERS

accepted The Paw with such fervor and it generated such enthusiasm and established such a unique and unmistakable identity for Clemson that naysayers quickly came aboard.

Today, Paw Power – the symbol of Clemson University -- reigns supreme on everything from highways to anything that can possibly be worn to caskets and car mufflers. The Paw is the ultimate ID card: Its wearer or bearer is a Clemson fan.

Who are you ?

You may not be Spider Man or the old Caped Crusader himself, but you do have a secret identity, don't you? It's hidden by the face you put on to meet the world each day, the expression that masks your secret longing to sail around the world or write a novel. Maybe you hide how much you hate your job or how badly you wish your spouse would lose weight.

You are, in fact, more than what you appear. The world does not know your depth, but you shouldn't feel too badly about the shortsightedness of others. Many people still can't figure out who Jesus is.

But that's not because Jesus failed to declare who he was; he told folks repeatedly. In like manner, what matters is not what others do not know about you but what they know for sure: That you are a Christian. That, above all else, should be your identity.

Deep inside, we're still the boys of autumn, that magic time of the year that once swept us on to America's fields.

-- Archie Manning.

**Many folks still don't know Jesus
for who he is, but everyone
should recognize you as one of his followers.**

GOOD SPORTS

Read Titus 2:1-8.

"Show integrity, seriousness and soundness of speech that cannot be condemned, so that those who oppose you may be ashamed because they have nothing bad to say about us" (vv. 7b, 8).

The early days of Clemson football provided some unique opportunities for good and bad sportsmanship.

The official records of the 1900 football season declare that Clemson beat Wofford 21-0. The margin of defeat was worse, though, than the score indicates. For one thing, touchdowns counted only five points. For another, before the game the players agreed that every touchdown Clemson scored after the first four would not count. The Tigers scored their allotted four in the game's first six minutes. After that, all Clemson touchdowns were called back, and Wofford got the ball deep in Tiger territory.

Later that season, the Clemson players experienced a painful example of extremely poor sportsmanship when they played Georgia in Athens (winning 39-5). Before the game, some students pelted the Tiger players with coal.

On Oct. 5, 1901, the Tigers rolled up the biggest score in school history with a 120-0 win over Guilford. The Tigers averaged thirty yards per play and scored a touchdown every 1:26. In a show of sportsmanship, though, they cut the first half to twenty minutes and the last half to ten to hold down the skyrocketing score.

TIGERS

Then in 1909 Clemson administrators revealed themselves to be rather poor sports when they had the entire football team arrested upon the players' return from a game. The team manager failed to obtain a permit for the team to leave the campus, and Coach Bob Williams decided to go ahead and board the train for Virginia. When the team returned, they were all arrested. The discipline committee showed some common sense and sportsmanship and cleared up the problem.

One of life's paradoxes is that many who would never consider cheating on the tennis court or the racquetball court to gain an advantage think nothing of doing so in other areas of their life. In other words, the good sportsmanship they practice on the golf course or even on the Monopoly board doesn't carry over. They play with the truth, cut corners, abuse others verbally, run rough-shod over the weaker, and generally cheat whenever they can to gain an advantage on the job or in their personal relationships.

But good sportsmanship is a way of living, not just of playing. Shouldn't you accept defeat without complaint (You don't have to like it.); win gracefully without gloating; treat your competition with fairness, courtesy, generosity, and respect? That's the way one team treats another in the name of sportsmanship. That's the way one person treats another in the name of Jesus.

One person practicing sportsmanship is better than a hundred teaching it.

-- Knute Rockne

Sportsmanship -- treating others with courtesy, fairness, and respect -- is a way of living, not just a way of playing.

FEAR FACTOR

Read Matthew 14:22-33.

"[The disciples] cried out in fear. But Jesus immediately said to them: 'Take courage! It is I. Don't be afraid'" (vv. 26-27).

When a player runs from the court in panic and the whole bench breaks into tears – this is a team that is afraid. It was the Clemson women's basketball team of 1999-2000.

That squad was one of the school's best, rolling up a 19-12 record and advancing to the second round of the NCAA Tournament. Thus, those Tigers weren't intimidated when they stepped onto the court. Still, they knew fear, the source of which was senior starting center Joanie Mungro.

On Dec. 4, 1999, in the game against Georgia Tech, Mungro turned and ran toward the Clemson bench, panicked from hyperventilation. Coach Jim Davis rushed to meet her as she passed out. When Mungro came to, Davis looked at his bench and couldn't find a dry eye. "They were all very concerned about Joanie," he said.

To calm those very real fears, Davis had the team physician speak to the Tigers and tell them exactly what to expect – because Joanie Mungro was playing with a pacemaker.

One Sunday in preseason during practice, Mungro felt as though she were having a heart attack. Tests revealed she had a rare defect that dropped her heart rate after exertion. A cardi-

TIGERS

ologist told her she needed a pacemaker. "I looked at him, and I was thinking, 'No way,'" Mungro said. "I am 23 years old. I do not need a pacemaker. I thought right then that basketball was over for me." But she did and it wasn't; the pacemaker allowed her to return to basketball, work her way into the starting lineup, average 24 minutes a game her senior season, and inspire all her teammates. "Almost like a second chance," Mungro said.

Even if it was scary for a while.

Some fears are universal; others are particular. Speaking to the Rotary Club may require a heavy dose of antiperspirant. Elevator walls may feel as though they're closing in on you. And don't even get started on being in the dark with spiders and snakes during a thunderstorm.

We all live in fear, and God knows this. Dozens of passages in the Bible urge us not to be afraid. God isn't telling us to lose our wariness of oncoming cars or big dogs with nasty dispositions; this is a helpful fear God instilled in us for protection.

What God does wish driven from our lives is a spirit of fear that dominates us, that makes our lives miserable and keeps us from doing what we should, such as sharing our faith. In commanding that we not be afraid, God reminds us that when we trust completely in him, we find peace that calms our fears.

Let me win. But if I cannot win, let me be brave in the attempt.
— Special Olympics Motto

**You have your own peculiar set of fears,
but they should never paralyze you
because God is greater than anything you fear.**

DAY 75

THE BIG TIME

Read Matthew 2:19-23.

"He went and lived in a town called Nazareth" (v. 23).

If anyone ever made the journey from the backwoods to the big time, it was Frank Howard.

On Dec. 10, 1969, Howard retired after 30 years as head coach of the Clemson football team. He won 165 games, the most in Tiger history. He won eight conference titles and was twice the ACC Coach-of-the-Year.

He remained at Clemson as athletic director until 1971 when he was named assistant to the vice-president of student affairs. Shortly after Howard's retirement, the college's trustees named the playing surface of Memorial Stadium "Frank Howard Field" in honor of his long service to the university. In 1989, Howard was inducted into the College Football Hall of Fame. He is a member of eleven other halls of fame including Clemson, the Orange Bowl, and the Gator Bowl. He received both the Order of the Palmetto, the highest order the governor of South Carolina can present, and the Clemson Medallion, the university's highest honor.

Frank Howard hit the big time.

But he sure didn't start out that way. He was born in Barlow Bend, Alabama, and once said his home town was "three wagon greasings from Mobile." His early years were spent on a farm; he couldn't play football because there weren't enough kids around.

TIGERS

Following Howard's retirement from coaching, a reporter tried to reach someone who might remember him growing up and was told by the Jackson Chamber of Commerce that Barlow Bend "isn't a very large town" and didn't have a mayor or a police department.

The "Baron of Barlow Bend" didn't start out in the big time; he just wound up there.

The move to the big time is one we often desire to make in our own lives. Bumps in the road, one stoplight communities, and towns with only a service station, a church, and a voting place litter the American countryside. Maybe you were born in one of them and grew up in a virtually unknown village in a backwater county. Perhaps you started out on a stage far removed from the bright lights of Broadway, the glitz of Hollywood, or the halls of power in Washington, D.C.

Those original circumstances don't have to define or limit you, though, for life is much more than geography. It is about character and walking with God whether you're in the countryside or the city. Jesus knew the truth of that. After all, he grew up in a small town in an inconsequential region of an insignificant country ruled by foreign invaders.

Where you are doesn't matter. What you are does.

Are you sure there is such a place?
-- Operator's reply when asked by a reporter to reach someone
in Barlow Bend

Where you live may largely be
the culmination of a series of circumstances;
what you are is a choice you make.

DAY 76

ANSWERING THE CALL

Read 1 Samuel 3:1-18.

"The Lord came and stood there, calling as at the other times, 'Samuel! Samuel!' Then Samuel said, 'Speak, for your servant is listening'" (v. 10).

Perhaps no one in Clemson football history has answered the call from his coaches as Bobby Hutchinson did.

Before his senior season of 2008 began, Hutchinson, an offensive lineman, had fallen far down the depth chart behind younger talent and wasn't expected to play much. Offensive line coach Brad Scott and head coach Tommy Bowden approached him about putting his playing days behind him and becoming a student assistant coach. Since Hutchinson had long dreamed of becoming a football coach and since the team needed him in a coaching capacity, he peeled off his pads and picked up a whistle, serving as Scott's assistant coach through the first four weeks of the season.

Injuries, however, ravaged the offensive line, and the coaches issued another call for Hutchinson: to make his first career start at left guard against Maryland. Hutchinson readily tossed his whistle aside. "We are so happy that he did come back," Bowden said. The Tigers rushed for 221 yards against the Terps, and Scott said it was "the best performance by the line this season."

When some of the injured linemen returned, Scott dutifully moved into a backup role, but he wasn't through answering the call. With three freshman linemen starting against Boston College in the eighth game of the season, the coaches needed the experienced Hutchinson on the field, so he started at center and went on to finish the season there. The Tigers closed with a 4-1 stretch and earned a Gator-Bowl bid. "We should have started that joker a long time ago," Coach Dabo Swinney said.

"There's no way I believed I'd ever get this chance," Hutchinson said. But he got his chance because he answered the call.

A team player is someone like Bobby Hutchinson who does whatever the coaches call upon him to do for the good of the team. Something quite similar occurs when God places a specific call upon a Christian's life.

This is much scarier, though, than shifting positions on a football team or volunteering to coach. The way many folks understand it is that answering God's call means going into the ministry, packing the family up, and moving halfway around the world to some place where folks have never heard of air conditioning, fried chicken, paved roads, or the Clemson Tigers. Zambia. The Philippines. Cleveland even.

Not for you, no thank you. And who can blame you?

But God usually calls folks to serve him where they are. In fact, God put you where you are right now, and he has a purpose in placing you there. Wherever you are, you are called to serve him.

It was like being in a foreign country.
-- Welsh soccer player Ian Rush on playing in Italy

**God calls you to serve him
right now right where you are.**

NOT WHAT THEY SEEM

Read Habakkuk 1:2-11.

"Why do you make me look at injustice? Why do you tolerate wrong? Destruction and violence are before me; there is strife, and conflict abounds" (v. 3).

All indications were that the Clemson basketball team of 1939 was robbed of a berth in the National Invitational Tournament – but things were not what they seemed.

The Tigers belonged to the 20-member Southern Conference back then, and ordinarily only the top eight teams were invited to the conference tournament. In 1939, however, eleven teams wound up in the tournament because five teams – including Clemson -- were tied for seventh and eighth places. A late bucket from Banks McFadden, Clemson's first basketball All-America, gave the Tigers a 44-43 win over North Carolina, which put them into the final eight against top-seeded Wake Forest.

Led again by McFadden, the Tigers pulled off a 30-28 upset. They then cruised past Davidson 49-33 in the semifinals and surprised Maryland 39-27 in the finals. The Tigers were the Southern Conference champions.

As such, the players expected an invitation to the NIT in those days before the NCAA Tournament. Instead, the invitation went to Maryland. McFadden said the players were so excited about the championship that they didn't really care too much, but weren't the Tigers robbed of an honor they deserved?

TIGERS

Years later, McFadden and teammate George Coakley learned that the team had indeed been invited to the NIT, but athletic director Jess Neely, who was also the football coach, had turned the tournament down. Neely said the "bread and butter" of Clemson athletics was football and since most of the basketball players were also on the football team, they needed to be at spring practice and not in New York City.

Sometimes in life – even in Clemson basketball -- things aren't what they seem. In our violent and convulsive times, we must confront the possibility of a new reality: that we are helpless in the face of anarchy; that injustice, destruction, and violence are pandemic in and symptomatic of our modern age. It seems that anarchy is winning, that the system of standards, values, and institutions we have cherished is crumbling while we watch.

But we should not be deceived or disheartened. God is in fact the arch-enemy of chaos, the creator of order and goodness and the architect of all of history. God is in control.

We often misinterpret history as the record of mankind's accomplishments -- which it isn't -- rather than the unfolding of God's plan -- which it is. That plan has a clearly defined end: God will make everything right. In that day things will be what they seem.

Nothing is ever as good as it seems or as bad as it seems.
                                          -- Former Clemson coach Curley Hallman

**The forces of good and decency often seem
helpless before evil's power, but don't be fooled:
God is in control and will set things right.**

DAY 78

ATTITUDE CHECK

Read 1 Thessalonians 5.

"Give thanks in all circumstances, for this is God's will for you in Christ Jesus" (v. 18).

"Coach, we need a change in attitude." That was basically the message fifth-year senior Wesley McFadden delivered to head coach Danny Ford.

Four weeks into the 1989 football season, the Clemson Tigers were undefeated, ranked seventh in the nation, and challengers for a national championship. But then came losses to Duke and Georgia Tech sandwiched around a win over Virginia. With undefeated and 12th-ranked N.C. State up next, the 5-2 Tigers faced the prospect of having their season completely unravel.

Ford admitted he "was at his wits' end" at what had happened to his team. The seniors met following the Tech loss, and after the meeting, McFadden "put a bug in the coach's ear."

"We weren't having fun," he said. "We were playing not to lose instead of playing to win." The seniors "told the coaches that the ACC championship was by the boards, to let's just go out and have fun and play with reckless abandonment."

Bob Bradley wrote, "The seniors' attitude changed this team's attitude." The Tigers smashed N.C. State 30-10. Ford recognized that the new attitude made all the difference, saying his team had probably been trying too hard. "It's just a tightness and sometimes you make more mistakes than you do when you go out and

TIGERS

have fun and just play," he said.

The new attitude didn't stop with the N.C. State game. The Tigers ripped Wake Forest 44-10, North Carolina 35-3, and South Carolina 45-0 and then rolled past West Virginia 27-7 in the Gator Bowl. The change in attitude carried the Tigers all the way to their third straight ten-win season, their fourth straight season with only two losses, and a No. 11 ranking.

How's your attitude? You can fuss because your house is not as big as some, because a coworker talks too much, or because you have to take pills every day. Or you can appreciate your home for providing warmth and shelter, the co-worker for the lively conversation, and the medicine for keeping you reasonably healthy.

Whether life is endured or enjoyed depends largely on your attitude. An attitude of thankfulness to God offers you the best chance to get the most out of your life because living in gratitude means you choose joy in your life no matter what your circumstances. This world does not exist to satisfy you, so chances are it will not. True contentment and joy are found in a deep, abiding relationship with God, and the proper way to approach God is not with haughtiness or anger but with gratitude for all he has given you.

I became an optimist when I discovered that I wasn't going to win any more games by being anything else.
-- Former major league manager Earl Weaver

Your attitude goes a long way
toward determining the quality of your life
and your relationship with God.

BE PREPARED

Read Matthew 10:5-23.

"I am sending you out like sheep among wolves. Therefore be as shrewd as snakes and as innocent as doves" (v. 16).

A book, a nail file – and a really good right arm – made Kris Benson the best college pitcher in the country in 1996.

The secret to Benson's success at Clemson lay in matching his exceptional talent with almost superhuman preparation. He prepared for the 1996 season by spending eight weeks in the weight room, which added 15 pounds of muscle to his body and several miles per hour to his fastball.

Despite all that physical preparation, Benson always insisted pitching was more brain than brawn, and therein lay the key to the intensity with which he prepared himself to pitch. Before every game, he pored over scouting reports. He kept a diary of each of his outings and studied a log that broke down every pitch he'd ever thrown. Always within a pitching arm's reach was a book with dog-eared and yellowed pages, *The Mental Game of Baseball*. "I've read that book backward and forward," Benson said.

Benson tended to every detail of his game. For instance, the day before each start, he carefully filed the nail of his right index finger down so he could wedge it between the baseball's seams. If the nail were too long, the curve wouldn't break; too short and it would break too much and be uncontrollable. "He's gotta have it just perfect," said his pitching coach, John Pawlowski.

All that preparation resulted in Benson's going 14-2 in 1996. He was the ACC Player of the Year, the ACC Athlete of the Year, and the National Player of the Year. He was the number one pick in the 1996 major league draft, the only Clemson athlete in history to be chosen number one in any draft.

Kris Benson always showed up prepared.

You know the importance of preparation in your own life. You went to the bank for a car loan, facts and figures in hand. That presentation you made at work was seamless because you practiced. The kids' school play suffered no meltdowns because they rehearsed. Knowing what you need to do and doing what you must to succeed isn't luck; it's preparation.

Jesus understood this, and he prepared his followers by lecturing them and by sending them on field trips. Two thousand years later, the life of faith requires similar training and study. You prepare so you'll be ready when that unsaved neighbor standing beside you at your backyard grill asks about Jesus. You prepare so you will know how God wants you to live. You prepare so you are certain in what you believe when the secular, godless world challenges it.

And one day you'll see God face to face. You certainly want to be prepared for that.

Spectacular achievements are always preceded by unspectacular preparation.

-- Roger Staubach

**Living in faith requires constant study
and training, preparation for the day
when you meet God face to face.**

UNEXPECTEDLY

Read Luke 2:1-20.

"She gave birth to her firstborn, a son. She wrapped him in cloths and placed him in a manger, because there was no room for them in the inn" (v. 7).

The most famous play of Harry Olszewski's illustrious football career was so unexpected and unplanned that he confesses to exactly what it was: an accident.

Olszewski is one of Clemson's greatest linemen ever. He was a guard on three straight ACC champions (1965-67). He was All-ACC as both a junior and a senior and was the only unanimous selection in 1967. He was also a consensus All-America his senior season, the year he won the ACC Jacobs Blocking Trophy as the best blocking lineman in the conference. In 1977, he was named to the Silver Anniversary All-ACC Team. He was inducted into the Clemson Hall of Fame in 1980 and the South Carolina Hall of Fame in 1990.

Olszewski remains a famous player in Clemson history, but he had fifteen minutes of fame that outshine all the others. In the 1966 35-10 win over South Carolina, Olszewski scored a touchdown, the last Clemson offensive lineman to do so. The Tigers were pounding USC with their favorite weapon, "student body left or right, our bread and butter," Olszewski said. "We must've run that eight million times in practice."

One time, though, when Olszewski turned to lead the sweep,

as he recalled it, his quarterback, Jimmy Addison, "must've mishandled the snap; there's the ball, just hovering in mid-air." So the quick-thinking Olszewski plucked the ball out of mid-air and turned upfield for a 12-yard touchdown run.

Unexpectedly, Olszewski had earned himself a niche in Clemson football history.

Just like Harry Olszewski who knew exactly what he was to do on that sweep against South Carolina, we think we've got everything figured out and planned for, and then something unexpected happens. Someone gets ill; you fall in love; you lose your job; you're going to have another child. Life surprises us with its bizarre twists and turns.

God is that way too, catching us unawares to remind us he's still around. A friend who hears you're down and stops by, a child's laugh, an achingly beautiful sunset -- unexpected moments of love and beauty. God is like that, always doing something in our lives we didn't expect.

But why shouldn't he? There is nothing God can't do. The only factor limiting what God can do is the paucity of our own faith.

Expect the unexpected from God, this same deity who unexpectedly came to live among us as a man. He does, by the way, expect a response from you.

Sports is about adapting to the unexpected and being able to modify plans at the last minute.
— Sir Roger Bannister, first-ever sub-four-minute miler

God does the unexpected to remind you
of his presence -- like showing up as Jesus –
and now he expects a response from you.

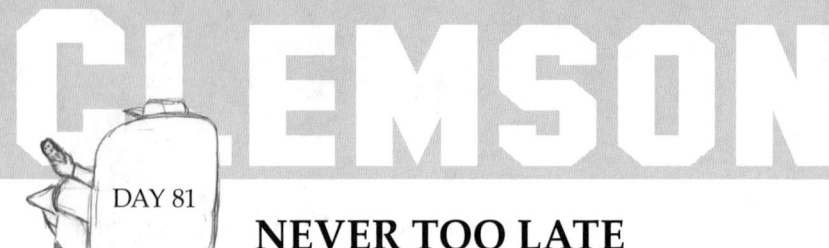

NEVER TOO LATE

Read Genesis 21:1-7.

"And [Sarah] added, 'Who would have said to Abraham that Sarah would nurse children? Yet I have borne him a son in his old age'" (v. 7).

Many Clemson students need extra time to complete their degrees. Few, however, can match former Tiger punter Mitch Tyner; he took almost 31 years to earn his degree.

After high school, Tyner punted for a junior college where he drew the attention of Clemson coach Red Parker, who signed him to a scholarship. His first punt at Clemson in 1973 was a disaster when the snap sailed over his head. He went on, though, to have a solid career. In 1973, he averaged 41.9 yards per punt, 12th best in the nation and second-best in the ACC. On Oct. 6, 1973 against Texas A&M, Tyner booted an 81-yard punt, a school record that still stands. In 1974, he averaged 40.1 yards per punt.

After a couple of NFL tryouts that didn't pan out, Tyner returned to the family farm in Darlington. He was just three credit hours short of his degree and had intentions of completing his coursework, but family responsibilities always came first. When his children began college, he started thinking again about his own education and setting a good example for them. "If they were going to school and getting their degree, I wanted to try to get mine," he said. "I should have done it a long time ago."

So Tyner went back to school with help from Clemson's football academic advisor, Joe White, who discovered Tyner could complete his degree by passing one independent study course. It wasn't as easy as it sounded because the course required the writing of a thesis and Tyner was certainly out of practice.

He persevered, though, and in the summer of 2002, more than 31 years after he began his college education, Mitch Tyner received his degree.

Running a marathon. Getting married. Starting a new career. Even getting that college degree. Though we may make all kinds of excuses, it's often never too late for life-changing decisions and milestones.

This is especially true in our faith life, which is based on God's promises. Abraham was 100 and Sarah was 90 when their first child was born. They were old folks even by the Bible's standards at the dawn of history. But God had promised them a child and just as God always does, he kept his promise no matter how unlikely it seemed.

God has made us all a promise of new life and hope through Jesus Christ. At any time in our lives – today even -- we can regret the things we have done wrong and the way we have lived, ask God in Jesus' name to forgive us for them, and discover a new way of living – forever.

It's never too late to change. God promised.

It's never too late to achieve success in sports.
-- Brooke de Lench, writer and lecturer on children and sports

It's never too late to change a life
by turning it over to Jesus.

HOMEBODIES

Read 2 Corinthians 5:1-10.

"We . . . would prefer to be away from the body and at home with the Lord" (v. 8).

Clemson felt like home, so the Tigers landed a key component of their national championship team and one of their greatest players ever.

Terry Kinard played for the Tigers from 1978-82, an injury in his first game forcing a redshirt year. He set a school record that still stands with 17 career interceptions. He was the second leading tackler on the national championship team of 1981 and the leading tackler on the 1982 squad that lost only one game and finished eighth in the nation.

He is Clemson's only two-time, first-team AP All-America, and CBS Sports named him the National Defensive Player of the Year in 1982. In 2001, he became the second Clemson player (Banks McFadden is the other.) to be inducted into the College Football Hall of Fame.

Asked once if Brett Favre were the best college player he ever coached, Curley Hallman, who coached linebackers and defensive backs at Clemson, said quite bluntly, "No. . . . A truly great player makes all those other people around him better players. They will play better than they are supposed to play." Kinard was the player for Hallman who did that better than anyone else.

Coming out of high school, though, Kinard was a lock to

play for South Carolina. He played for Sumter High and grew up watching Gamecock football. His dream was to play football in Columbia. The recruiting process changed that, much to the eternal rejoicing of Clemson fans.

Kinard said he had "a bad experience" on his visit to Columbia. "It wasn't a situation I wanted to be in," he said. Clemson, however, was altogether different. "It felt like home," Kinard said. "The players seemed like decent guys."

Terry Kinard felt at home in Clemson and thus did the school land the most decorated football player in its history.

Home is not necessarily a matter of geography. It may be that place you share with your spouse and your children, whether it's South Carolina or Texas. You may feel at home when you return to Clemson, wondering why you were so eager to leave in the first place. Maybe the home you grew up in still feels like an old shoe, a little worn but comfortable and inviting.

God planted that sense of home in us because he is a God of place, and our place is with him. Thus, we may live a few blocks away from our parents and grandparents or we may relocate every few years, but we will still sometimes feel as though we don't really belong no matter where we are. We don't; our true home is with God in the place Jesus has gone ahead to prepare for us. We are homebodies and we are perpetually homesick.

Everybody's better at home.
— Basketball player Justin Dentmon

We are continually homesick for our real home,
which is with God in Heaven.

IT'S THE TRUTH

Read Matthew 5:33-37.

*"Simply let your 'Yes' be 'Yes,' and your 'No,' 'No';
anything beyond this comes from the evil one" (v. 37).*

Billy Luckie lied to his mama.

His teammates viewed the redshirt freshman as a "quiet, almost subdued backup quarterback." But everything changed on Sept. 28, 1996, when starting quarterback Nealon Greene went down with a sprained knee on the first play of the second quarter against Wake Forest. "Billy got on that field and doggone he came alive," said center Jamie Trimble. "You could see it in his eye."

The players apparently could also hear it in his voice. "They said I was just yelling at the top of my lungs," Luckie recalled. "Guys were like, 'Shh, shh. Be quiet. Calm down.'" Luckie then promptly overadjusted the volume. "Then they came back the next time and told me to yell it at the line of scrimmage because they weren't hearing me real well," Luckie said.

Interestingly, a Wake Forest player helped Luckie settle his nerves. When he walked to the line for his first play, a Wake linebacker whom Luckie had played against in high school and knew started yapping, "Heeey, Luckie-Luckie-Luckie!" "I just started smiling and laughing," he said.

Three plays into his first series, Luckie threw his first collegiate pass: He hit Kenya Crooks for a 33-yard gain. From that moment, the game belonged to him. He completed 8 of 11 passes for 91 yards and led the Tigers to a 21-10 win.

That tale Luckie told his mama -- it certainly wasn't intentional; he was just a lousy prognosticator. The night before the game he talked to his parents. His dad was seeking a couple of extra tickets, and Luckie's mother asked him if he'd play. He told her, "No way. This is supposed to be a tight game and I'm not going to play. You'll be better off just watching it on TV." When he talked to his mom after the game, she told him she was never listening to him again.

No, that dress doesn't make you look fat. But, officer, I wasn't speeding. I didn't get the project finished because I've been at the hospital every night with my ailing grandmother. What good-looking guy? I didn't notice.

Sometimes we lie to spare the feelings of others; more often, though, we lie to bail ourselves out of a jam, to make ourselves look better to others, or to gain the upper hand over someone.

But Jesus admonishes us to tell the truth. Frequently in our faith life we fret about what is right and what is wrong, but we can have no such ambivalence when it comes to telling the truth or lying. God and his son are so closely associated with the truth that lying is ultimately attributed to the devil ("the evil one"). Given his character, God cannot lie; given his character, the devil lies as a way of life. Given your character, which is it?

Trampling on the truth has become as common place as overpaid athletes and bad television.

-- *Hockey coach Dan Bauer*

**Jesus declared himself to be the truth,
so whose side are we on when we lie?**

BODYWORK

Read 1 Corinthians 6:12-20.

"Do you not know that your body is a temple of the Holy Spirit, who is in you, whom you have received from God? . . . Honor God with your body" (vv. 19, 20b).

Opposing coaches called it a coal mine, a sweat box, a snake pit, and a cow palace – and that's when they were being polite.

"It" was Fike Field House, the home of Clemson basketball from 1930 until 1968. While other home courts may have hosted more successful teams, no facility was ever as wild or as downright crazy as Fike. Or perhaps as unusual.

Coaches didn't call it "a coal mine" for no reason. Fike was dark. Longtime Wake Forest coach Bones McKinney said the place was "so-o-o dark that the referees had to come in wearing coal miners' helmets." Clemson All-American Banks McFadden said, "The bricks were dark, the wood floor was dark, the lights were poor."

Another of Fike's unusual features was a live steam pipe that ran around the top of the seats. The teams had to sit on the first row of the bleachers, which meant they were part of the crowd. Oh, yes, the Fike crowd. "There was nothing but dark, and all you could hear was the crowd roaring – louder and louder," recalled McKinney. "You could never run away from the crowd there."

The crowd was so close to the court that officials used people's feet for out-of-bounds marks. McKinney recalled that the Clem-

TIGERS

son cadets would "pluck the hair out of our players' legs when they tried to throw the ball in."

The clocks were so high up that players couldn't see them from all places on the floor, and so many lights were usually burned out that they "resembled a flashing Christmas decoration in a small town firehouse."

Fike Field House clearly left something to be desired compared to today's palatial arenas.

Your body may not be as peculiar looking as Fike was, but most of us still don't see a perfect facility or a body beautiful when we look into a mirror. Too heavy, too short, too pale, too gray — there's always something wrong because we compare ourselves to an impossible standard Hollywood and fashion magazines have created, and we are inevitably disappointed.

God must have been quite partial to your body, though, because he personally fashioned it and gave it to you free of charge. Your body, like everything else in your life, is thus a gift from God.

But God didn't stop there. He then quite voluntarily chose to inhabit your body, sharing it with you in the person of the Holy Spirit. What an act of consummate ungratefulness it is then to abuse your God-given body by violating God's standards for living. To do so is in fact to dishonor God.

If you don't do what's best for your body, you're the one who comes up on the short end.

-- Julius Erving

**You may not have a fine opinion of your body,
but God thought enough of it
to personally create it for you.**

MAKING PLANS

Read Psalm 33:1-15.

"The plans of the Lord stand firm forever, the purposes of his heart through all generations" (v. 11).

Though they were ranked No. 1, the Tigers were underdogs to fourth-ranked Nebraska in the 1982 Orange Bowl. But Coach Danny Ford had a plan.

Ford's strategy to overcome the advantage Nebraska had with its superior size and strength centered on being ready for the Miami weather. Ford had his Tigers in Florida early, and he proceeded to put them "through a brutal barrage of drills." The Tigers ran 40-yard dashes and "drills at breakneck speed without pads. They ran until some of them were at the point of vomiting."

The wisdom of Ford's approach revealed itself before the first kickoff. Game night in Miami the temperature was 77 degrees with 74-percent humidity. Nose tackle William Devane looked across at the Nebraska players during warmups and saw that the "Nebraska players, who were warming up without their pads, . . . were wringing, soaking wet with sweat. Clemson's players had pads on and were barely sweating."

The conditions cost the Tigers. Defensive tackle Dan Benish lost thirteen pounds, and quarterback Homer Jordan fainted when the game ended. But the Cornhuskers had it worse. In the second quarter Benish saw Nebraska center Dave Rimington struggling to catch his breath. Benish and fellow defensive tackle Jeff Bryant "felt great."

Benish said of Nebraska that in the fourth quarter, at crunch time with Clemson hanging on to a 22-15 lead, the Huskers "ran out of steam. . . . They couldn't come off the line. They couldn't do anything."

Danny Ford's plan worked to perfection: 12-0 perfection, in fact.

Successful living, like winning a football game, takes planning. You go to school to improve your chances for a better paying job. You use blueprints to build your home. You plan for retirement. You map out your vacation to have the best time. You even plan your children -- sometimes.

Your best-laid plans, however, sometimes get wrecked by events and circumstances beyond your control. The economy goes into the tank; a debilitating illness strikes; a hurricane hits. Life is capricious and thus no plans -- not even your best ones -- are foolproof.

But you don't have to go it alone. God has plans for your life that guarantee success as God defines it if you will make him your planning partner. God's plan for your life includes joy, love, peace, kindness, gentleness, and faithfulness, all the elements necessary for truly successful living for today and for all eternity. And God's plan will not fail.

If you don't know where you are going, you will wind up somewhere else.

-- *Yogi Berra*

Your plans ensure a successful life;
God's plans ensure a successful eternity.

DAY 86

HOW WE LEAVE

Read 2 Kings 2:1-12.

"A chariot of fire and horses of fire appeared and separated the two of them, and Elijah went up to heaven in a whirlwind" (v. 11).

Frank Howard didn't exactly choose when he stepped down as Clemson's head football coach, but he did choose how he left.

On Dec. 10, 1969, after 39 years of coaching at Clemson – 30 of them as the head coach – Howard resigned. He said "he had to quit coaching because of health reasons – 'the alumni got sick of me.'" This was just one of Howard's many classic lines, but it contained some truth. The Clemson legend, who said his original aim in life was to go to Auburn and be a chicken farmer and that he became a coach because he got to take a shower every day, didn't really pick the terms under which he left. He said he had "made the decision last April or May to resign," but sportswriter Herman Helms was among the many who saw the truth.

Helms said that Howard "tried to make it look right, for Clemson's sake," but "the timing was the giveaway. No coach plans to quit three days before the signing date for high school recruits . . . particularly if his successor is not at his side." Helms said, "An old warrior left because things had become so unpleasant for him. . . . A contributor who gave so much to a game and a school and a state left because people have short memories. . . . It was sad. There is no other way to say it." Helms wrote, "It would have been nice" if Howard had been the one to pick the time to leave, "but it didn't happen that way."

Howard could well have lashed out at his critics, but he chose instead to leave "without rancor, without bitterness." After all, he would never do anything to hurt his beloved Clemson. He left with grace and class, a man of integrity and loyalty to the last moment.

Like Frank Howard and Elijah, we can't always choose the exact circumstances under which we leave.

You probably haven't always chosen the moves you've made in your life. Perhaps your company transferred you. A landlord didn't renew your lease. An elderly parent needed your care.

Sometimes the only choice we have about leaving is the manner in which we go, whether we depart with style and grace or not. Our exit from life is the same way. Unless we usurp God's authority over life and death, we can't choose how we die, just how we handle it. Perhaps the most frustrating aspect of dying is that we have at most very little control over the process. As with our birth, our death is in God's hands. We finally must surrender to his will even if we have spent a lifetime refusing to do so.

We do, however, control our destination. How we leave isn't up to us; where we spend eternity is -- and that depends on our relationship with Jesus.

How can football become so cruelly competitive that a contributor such as Frank Howard cannot pick his own time to go?
-- Sportswriter Herman Helms

When you go isn't up to you; where you go is.

DAY 87

LIVE ACTION

Read James 2:14-26.

"Faith by itself, if it is not accompanied by action, is dead"
(v. 17).

What in the world did Coach Tommy West tell his football
team at halftime that turned a 14-13 deficit into a 47-21 romp over
South Carolina?

When a reporter asked him that question after the 1997 win,
West answered, "It was the greatest talk I've ever given the team.
. . . It was an unbelievable talk. And it worked." West was having
a laugh at the reporters' expense because in reality what he told
his team was very little. He gave no rousing, legendary "win-
one-for-the-Gipper" pep talk, no over-the-top emotional plea.
West knew talk might help iron out some difficulties but it wasn't
going to win the game. What was needed was action.

And the Tigers delivered the action, "a 27-point barrage in
the third quarter that was the backbone of a 44-point flurry of
unanswered scoring that left the Gamecocks (5-6) flat, broke and
busted."

The action came quickly in the third quarter. Cornerback
Antwan Edwards' interception led to Nealon Greene's touchdown pass to wide receiver Tony Horne. Then in only 1:59 of the
quarter, Horne returned a punt 39 yards for a score and Edwards
returned his second interception 42 yards for a TD. The lead
was up to 33-14. Greene tossed a 15-yard touchdown pass to Mal

174   DAY 87

Lawyer before Javis Austin's 19-yard scoring romp wrapped up the last-half explosion. With his two scoring tosses, Greene set the Clemson season record of 16 touchdown passes.

Tailback Raymond Priester, who rushed for 112 yards on 24 carries, said most of the halftime talk was about blocking schemes. As West said, "We didn't change anything." But Priester said that West did tell his players they had only 30 more minutes: "Either 30 more minutes of football for the year, or 30 more minutes until a bowl game." That was it.

The talk over, the action followed.

Talk is cheap. Consider your neighbor or coworker who talks without saying anything, who makes promise she doesn't keep, who brags about his own exploits, who can always tell you how to do something but never shows up for the work.

How often have you fidgeted through a meeting, impatient to get on with the work everybody is talking about doing? You know – just as Tommy West and his Clemson Tigers knew against South Carolina -- that speech without action just doesn't cut it.

That principle applies in the life of a person of faith too. Merely declaring our faith isn't enough, however sincere we may be. It is putting our faith into action that shouts to the world of the depth of our commitment to Christ. Just as Jesus' ministry was a virtual whirlwind of activity, so are we to change the world by doing.

Jesus calls us to do more than talk a good game.

Don't talk too much or too soon.

-- Bear Bryant

Faith that does not reveal itself in action is dead.

THE GREATEST

Read Mark 9:33-37.

"If anyone wants to be first, he must be the very last, and the servant of all" (v. 35).

In keeping with a program that is one of the best in the nation, Clemson has had more than its share of sensational baseball pitchers. The greatest of them all, though, may still be Billy O'Dell.

O'Dell pitched for the Tigers from 1952-54, leading them to the Southern Conference championship in 1953 and the championship of the brand new Atlantic Coast Conference in 1954. Bobby Morris, who caught O'Dell both in high school and at Clemson, said Billy was "like a radio. Plug him in and he comes on." Since the Tigers played only 63 games during his three varsity seasons, O'Dell won only 19 games, far from the school record of 44, held by Brian Barnes (1986-89).

But his name is still all over the Clemson record book. He holds the record for best ERA for a season (0.79), and a career (1.51). He is the Tiger strikeout leader for a game (21 against South Carolina in 1952) and holds the record for strikeouts per nine innings for a season (13.4) and a career (12.3). He also is the Clemson record-holder for fewest hits per nine innings pitched for a season (3.11) and a career (5.29).

On May 8, 1953, O'Dell no-hit South Carolina, facing only 28 batters in that seven-inning game. Only two balls were hit to the outfield. Perhaps his biggest night ever, though, was that 21-K performance against South Carolina. He started out hot – fanning the first five batters – and finished hot, striking out the final five. He struck out the sides four times and even fanned four batters in one inning thanks to a passed ball.

Billy O'Dell was the greatest, even once being appointed coach for a game when head coach Bob Smith was injured.

We all want to be the greatest. For instance, the goal for the baseball Tigers and their fans every season is Omaha and the College World Series. The competition at work is to be the most productive sales person on the staff or the Teacher of the Year. In other words, we define being the greatest in terms of the struggle for personal success. It's nothing new; the disciples saw greatness in the same way.

As Jesus illustrated, though, greatness in the Kingdom of God has nothing to do with the world's understanding of success. Rather, the greatest are those who channel their ambition toward the furtherance of Christ's kingdom through love and service, rather than their own advancement, which is a complete reversal of status and values as the world sees them.

After all, who could be greater than the person who has Jesus for a brother and God for a father? And that's every one of us.

My goal was to be the greatest athlete that ever lived.
-- Babe Didrikson Zaharias

To be great for God has nothing to do
with personal advancement and everything to do
with the advancement of Christ's kingdom.

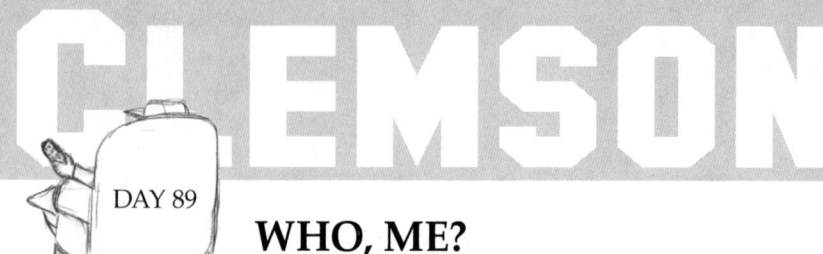

DAY 89

WHO, ME?

Read Judges 6:11-23.

"'But Lord,' Gideon asked, 'how can I save Israel? My clan is the weakest in Manasseh, and I am the least in my family'" (v. 15).

The Dallas Cowboys hit Clemson receiver Charlie Waters with a question so odd that the only logical answer was "Who, me?"

As a junior in 1968, Waters started at quarterback for the Tigers when projected starter Billy Ammons was injured. The defending ACC champs started 0-3-1; Waters later admitted that he wasn't a great quarterback. When Ammons returned, he took over the starting role, and Waters shifted to split end, where he found a home. He was All-ACC in 1969.

The Green Bay Packers told Waters on draft day 1970 they planned to select him with their third-round pick. Thus, Waters – for at least a fleeting moment – had visions of catching passes from legendary Packer quarterback Bart Starr. But the Dallas Cowboys picked ahead of Green Bay and chose Waters.

Then came the phone call with the surprising question: "You think you can backpedal?" Not exactly the question a wide receiver would expect. Stunned, Waters managed to come up with the answer that launched his professional career: yes. The Cowboys moved him into the defensive backfield even though, as Waters said, "I had never made a tackle in my life, except high school, until I got to the NFL."

He was a natural, making the 1970 NFL all-rookie team as a free safety before settling in at strong safety and becoming one of the best defensive players of the decade. He appeared in three Pro Bowls and five Super Bowls, helping to win two of them.

Even his former teammates shared his surprise at the Cowboys' question. "We kind of laughed" about Waters playing defense, Ammons said. But they weren't as surprised as Waters was when he got that fateful phone call.

You probably know exactly how Charlie Waters felt; you've experienced that moment of unwelcome surprise with its sinking "who, me?" feeling. How about that time the teacher called on you when you hadn't done a lick of homework? Or the night the hypnotist pulled you out of a room full of folks to be his guinea pig? You've had the wide-eyed look and the turmoil in your midsection when you were suddenly singled out and found yourself in a situation you neither sought nor were prepared for.

You may feel the same way Gideon did about being called to serve God in some way, quailing at the very notion of being audacious enough to teach Sunday school, lead a small group study, or coordinate a high school prayer club. After all, who's worthy enough to do anything like that?

The truth is that nobody is – but that doesn't seem to matter to God. And it's his opinion, not yours, that counts.

Surprise me.
           -- Yogi Berra on where his wife should have him buried.

**You're right in that no one is worthy to serve God,
but the problem is that doesn't matter to God.**

THE PRIZE

Read Philippians 3:10-16.

"I press on toward the goal to win the prize for which God has called me heavenward in Christ Jesus" (v. 14).

A Clemson sports publicity man once worked overtime to keep a Tiger football player from making All-America.

In 1939, Joe Sherman's job was to secure all the favorable publicity he could for Clemson's players, and the choicest plum of all was a spot on an All-American team. In mid-October of that year, Sherman received a letter from a publication's editor informing him that Banks McFadden, still regarded by many as Clemson's greatest athlete ever, had been selected for their All-American team.

The problem for Sherman, however, was that the all-star team was Little All-America, conceived "to pay honor to outstanding players at small colleges." Those were the days when every time the Tigers defeated Tulane, George Washington, Navy or similar powerhouses, the papers would refer to "Little Clemson." "I never got so sick of one descriptive phrase in my life," Sherman said.

So he wrote the editor and thanked him profusely for the compliment he wanted to pay McFadden. He then begged him not to do it. Sherman said that Clemson played big-time football and McFadden was good enough to make the Associated Press All-American team. Being picked on the "little" team would doom McFadden's chances of receiving the honor he deserved.

The editor replied, "I think you're nuts. Your boy doesn't have a ghost of a chance to make the big All-Americas." But he honored Sherman's request.

Sherman's reluctance to promote McFadden for the "little" team was justified when "Bonnie" Banks made enough of the major all-star teams to be a consensus All-America.

Even the most modest and self-effacing among us can't help but be pleased by prizes and honors. They symbolize the approval and appreciation of others, whether it's an All-American team, an Employee of the Month plaque, a Most Improved Player trophy, or the sign declaring yours as the neighborhood's prettiest yard.

Such prizes and awards are often the culmination of the pursuit of personal achievement and accomplishment. They represent accolades and recognition from the world. Nothing is inherently wrong with any of that as long as we keep them in perspective.

That is, we must never let such awards become idols that we worship or lower our sight from the greatest prize of all and the only one truly worth winning. It's one that won't rust, collect dust, or leave us wondering why we worked so hard to win it in the first place. The ultimate prize is eternal life, and it's ours through Jesus Christ.

A gold medal is a wonderful thing, but if you're not enough without it, you'll never be enough with it.
                                        -- John Candy in Cool Running

**The greatest prize of all doesn't require
competition to claim it;
God has it ready to hand to you.**

CLEMSON

NOTES
(Devotional Day Number)

1   "This country is in wretched . . . the college was renamed Clemson University.: "About Clemson: History," http://www.clemson.edu.about/history, Feb. 24, 2009.

1   he had played as an undergraduate at Auburn.: Lou Sahadi, *The Clemson Tigers* (New York: William Morrow & Co., Inc., 1983), p. 7.

1   On Sept. 30, 1986,: Sam Blackman et al, Clemson: *Where the Tigers Play* (Champaign, IL: Sports Publishing, LLC, 2001), p. 2.

1   a group of 30 students met . . a football aid association.: Sahadi, p. 7.

1   They asked Professor Riggs to coach the school's first football team.: Blackman, p. 2.

1   Twenty-one students began practice : Sahadi, p. 7.

1   on Oct. 5. . . . go all over campus.": Blackman, p. 3.

2   The Tigers were scheduled to open . . . were a last-minute replacement..: "Clemson Tigers: Traditions: National Championship," http://clemsontigers.cstv.com/sports/m-footbl/spec-rel/021809aab.html, Feb. 25, 2009.

2   The win failed . . . in the top 20.: "Clemson Tigers: National Championship."

2   "despicable, vile, unprincipled scoundrels.": John MacArthur, *Twelve Ordinary Men* (Nashville: W Publishing Group, 2002), p. 152.

3   "prettiest thunderstorm ever." Blackman, p. 260.

3   the rules then required . . . be restarted from scratch.: Blackman, p. 260.

3   Harold Stowe then pitched the game of his career,: Blackman, p. 261.

4   "I thought it was his hamstring . . . "He shook it off,": Justin A. Rice, "Spiller Delivers Knockout Blow," *The State*, Nov. 2, 2008, http://docs.newsbank.com/s/InfoWeb/aggdocs/NewsBank/12434A3FE4C4F2D8, May 6, 2009.

4   "Twenty-eight was the difference down the stretch for sure,": Rice.

4   Even if he had been in pain, . . . I was ready to go.": Rice.

4   Sometimes you have to play with a little pain.: Rice.

5   "I'm really different," . . . It would be a nightmare.": Lezlie Patterson, "ACC Tournament Awaits Clemson," *The State*, April 19, 1991, http://docs.newsbank.com/s/InfoWeb/aggdocs/NewsBank/0F0F83951E95147C, May 4, 2009.

5   After a disappointing sophomore . . . her coach growing up.: Patterson, "ACC Tournament Awaits."

6   before a big game . . . meat brought to his players.: Tysiac, Ken, *Tales from Clemson's 1981 Championship Season* (Champaign, IL: Sports Publishing L.L.C., 2006), p. 12.

6   when offensive line coach Larry . . . reveal it was all a gag.: Tysiac, *Tales*, pp. 6, 8.

6   While some declined, many . . . put limitations on yourselves.: Tysiac, *Tales*, p. 12.

7   At the postgame news conference, . . . to have your season end,": Steve Kirk, "Tigers Go for NIT Glory," *The State*, March 25, 1999, http://docs.newsbank.com/s/InfoWeb/aggdocs/NewsBank/0EB587E93001957A, May 5, 2009.

TIGERS

7   "how to smile again. How . . . the most of what we've got,": Kirk, "Tigers Go for NIT Glory."

8   The "mystical powers" of Howard's Rock.: Blackman, p. 57.

8   In the early 1950s, a Clemson graduate . . . make their famous entrance.: Sahadi, p. 69.

8   The football players did not begin . . . down the hill until 1967,: Blackman, p. 57.

8   "It was obvious some kind . . . on this particular day.": Blackman, p. 57.

8   The superstitious Howard once told . . . been a lot better coach.": Sahadi, pp. 69-70.

9   He had a wire fence . . . at all future Clemson games.: Joe Sherman, *Clemson Tigers* (Columbia: The R.L. Bryan Company, 1976), p. 53.

10   Senior associate athletic director . . . He then turned to Davis,: Lezlie Patterson, "Earning His Stripes," *The State*, March 7, 1992, http://docs.newsbank.com/s/InfoWeb/aggdocs/NewsBank/0F0F839C8388EFF5, May 4, 2009.

10   "approaches his job like a math . . . a subject matter to teach.": Patterson, "Earning His Stripes."

11   Bethea was recruited by only . . . have a better chance to play.": Carl Martin, *Real Champions: Tigers Touched by God* (Pickens, S.C.: E.P.I.C. Publishing, 2001), p. 51.

11   He was on the scout team . . . and I did fully recover.": Martin, p. 52.

11   If you put forth the effort, God will be there to help.: Martin, p. 53.

12   "This won't take long. . . . as tough as nails.": Blackman, p. 263.

12   "Charles is a tough, tough nut. . . . before he made some birdies.": Blackman, p. 263.

13   "When the committee was interviewing . . . I don't fear anybody.": Sahadi, p. 124.

13   a newspaper article described him . . . prove 'em wrong first.": Sahadi, p. 127.

13   "ugly whispers were heard . . . had to win and win big.": Sahadi, p. 128.

14   "I just want everybody to know that I don't think it's right,": Sahadi, p. 95.

14   "It was like I woke up . . . harsher than we expected.": Sahadi, p. 96.

15   the starting quarterback, Richard Moncrief, . . . in only one college football game.: Bob Gillespie, "Solomon Proves a Wise Decision," *The State*, Oct. 11, 1992, http://docs.newsbank.com/s/InfoWeb/aggdocs/NewsBank/0F0F822A01ABB365, May 4, 2009.

15   "Louis was the spark," . . . to key another touchdown drive.: Gillespie, "Solomon Proves."

15   the greatest comeback in school history.: Gillespie, "Solomon Proves."

16   "We were all excited about what she would do this season,": Lorie Johnson, "Heart Breaker," *Sharing the Victory Magazine*, Nov. 2006, http://www.sharingthevictory.com/vsItemDisplay.1sp&objectID=D3B21789, April 30, 2009.

16   In May 2006, Ross collapsed . . . to point others to Christ.: Johnson.

17   Young and golfer Jonathan Byrd . . . All-America in all three areas.: "Kyle Young, Profile," http://clemsontigers.cstv.com/genrel/young_kyle00.html, June 14, 2009.

17   The coaches "require you . . . If you're not, you pay for it.": Steve Kirk, "Clemson's Young Proves It Can Be Done," *The*

State, Oct. 16, 1998, http://docs.newsbank.com/s/InfoWeb/aggdocs/
NewsBank/0EB5878CBA49B485, May 5, 2009.

18   "when players and coaches could . . . still be friends offcourt.": Blackman, p. 36.

18   "It was a different time back then," . . . time to look back on.": Blackman, p. 37.

18   Press Maravich (1956-62) would always . . . the court wouldn't change that.": Blackman, p. 36.

18   Frank Howard said the relationships . . . other coaches being a pall-bearer,": Blackman, p. 41.

18   Everything gets better as the years go by.: Blackman, p. 39.

19   In January 2003 on a FOX . . . nipped at the finish line.: "Shawn Crawford," *Wikipedia, the free encyclopedia*, http://en.wikipedia.org/wiki/Shawn_Crawford, June 10, 2009.

19   out-leaned at the finish line . . . I didn't deserve the medal.": Scott Fowler, "Silver a Bitter Prize for Former Tiger," *The State*, Aug. 21, 2008, http://docs.newsbank.com/s/InfoWeb/aggdocs/NewsBank/122B3B93902218B0, May 6, 2009.

20   Before Neely left for Rice . . . all you'll ever need.": "Clemson Tigers: Facilities: Memorial Stadium," http://clemsontigers.cstv.com/school-bio/facilities-football.html, Feb. 25, 2009.

20   But Neely was barely in Texas . . . west of Riggs Field.: Bob Bradley, *Death Valley Days* (Atlanta: Longstreet Press, 1991), p. 11.

20   Two members of the football team . . . mules and a scoop.: Bradley, p. 12.

20   "The gates were hung at 1:00 and we played at 2:00.": "Clemson Tigers: Facilities."

20   "storied edifice": "Clemson Tigers: Facilities."

21   Clemson led 10-9 at halftime . . . went berserk and punched Bauman.: Bradley, p. 98.

21   "a purely selfish matter . . . misfortune or frustration": Bruce T. Dahlberg, "Anger," *The Interpreter's Dictionary of the Bible* (Nashville: Abingdon Press, 1962), Vol. 1, p. 136.

22   "set the standards for all Lady Tigers on and off the court.": "Barbara Kennedy-Dixon: Profile," http://clemsontigers.cstv.com/sports/w-baskbl/mtt/kennedydixon_barbara00.html, June 16, 1009.

22   came to Clemson on a volleyball . . . had no basketball scholarships left.: "Barbara Kennedy-Dixon: Profile."

23   Tears mingled with chuckles: Josh Peter, "Tears Mix with Chuckles at Services for Howard," *The State*, Jan. 29, 1996, http://docs.newsbank.com/s/InfoWeb/aggdocs/NewsBank/0EB58503BB886F90, May 5, 2009.

23   he could spend all eternity there, "listening to the cheers for my Tigers,": Sahadi, p. 71.

23   Though it was a bright . . . and everybody clapped along.: Amanda Mays, "Tigers' 'Rock of Ages,'" *The State*, Jan. 29, 1996, http://docs.newsbank.com/s/InfoWeb/aggdocs/NewsBank/0EB58503B585AFBB, May 5, 2009.

23   "Frank Howard was Clemson.": Bob Spear, "Love Him, Hate Him, But Never Forget Him," *The State*, Jan. 27, 1996, http://docs.newsbank.com/s/InfoWeb/aggdocs/NewsBank/0F0F82EfFA7E5728, May 5, 2009.

24   "shunned by other schools because of his smallness,": Sherman, p. 56.

24   Coach Jess Neely was reluctant . . . who had scouted Carolina,: Sherman, p. 57.

24   asked him if Grygo were better . . . Shad started the next game: Sherman, p. 58.

25   "It" was the elbow of . . . headaches, dizziness, and blurred vision.: Bob Cole, "Tigers' Hines Trying to Keep Perspective," *The State*, March 7, 1993, http://docs.newsbank.com/s/InfoWeb/aggdocs/NewsBank/0F0F8233B158 D716, May 4, 2009.

26   "probably the best, if not the best," football player" he ever had,: Blackman, p. 227.

26   Cone's strange odyssey to . . . visited his sister in Biloxi.: Blackman, p. 226.

26   She lived next door to . . . as the 40th name.: Blackman, p. 227.

26   whom Sports Information Director . . . named his recruiting coordinator: Blackman, p. 227.

26   On that fateful visit Cone . . . he just looked so athletic.": Blackman, p. 229.

27   The week before the Hall of Fame . . . "No. 1 defense in the nation.": Bob Gillespie, "Country's Top 'D'?" *The State*, Jan. 2, 1991, http://docs.newsbank.com/s/InfoWeb/aggdocs/NewsBank/0F0F82A521FFF0D7, May 4, 2009.

27   "They said we hadn't . . . didn't have a lifeguard's chance.": Gillespie, "Country's Top 'D'?"

28   Burnham's immediate response to the . . . to expect along the way.": Mark R. McCallum, "Burnham Gets Bounce Back in His Step," *The State*, March 31, 1995, http://docs.newsbank.com/s/InfoWeb/aggdocs/ NewsBank/0EB5845AE8A7B5E5, May 4, 2009.

28   "Every day, I come out . . . watching everyone else have fun.": McCallum.

28   "You look at life differently after you've been in the cellar health-wise,": McCallum.

29   Howard dubbed him "Dumb Dumb" . . . the wrong way on offense.: Bradley, p. 66.

29   In Clemson's 34-0 shellacking . . . he's going to kill [us] all.": Josh Peter, "Simmons Newest Pupil at Tigers' Linebacker U," *The State*, Sept. 21, 1996, http://docs.newsbank.com/s/infoWeb/aggdocs/NewsBank/0EB585C1F66 260D4, May 5, 2009.

29   Jackie Calvert went 81 yards . . . got everybody into the game.: Bradley, p. 66.

30   Often at practice, when they . . . just run to the corner.": Tysiac, *Tales*, p. v.

30   Jordan told Tuttle to be ready.: Tysiac, *Tales*, p. 41.

30   Jordan surveyed the defense . . . The fade was coming: Tysiac, *Tales*, p. 150.

30   "a perfect strike, a great ball to catch,": Tysiac, *Tales*, pp. 150-51.

30   "I just laid it up, and he went and got it,": Tysiac, *Tales*, p. 42.

30   the only one ever to feature a Clemson athlete in action.: Tysiac, *Tales*, p. 151.

30   "a hero forever to . . . the issue to autograph.": Trisha Lucey, "Perry Tuttle, Clemson Wide Receiver," *Sports Illustrated*, Dec. 14, 1998, http://vault.sportsillustrated.cnn.com/vault/article/magazine/MAG1014771/index.htm, Feb. 26, 2009.

30   More than twenty years later, . . . are they coming from?": Tysiac, *Tales*, p. 43.

31   "rivals any miracle in NCAA sports.": "Tigers Come on

Strong Late in the Season," *Clemson Tigers: Men's Soccer: 1987 National Championship,* http://clemsontigers.cstv.com/sports/m-soccer/spec-rel/060203aab.html, April 15, 2009.

31   "the national championship was not a realistic goal.": "Tigers Come on Strong."

31   "Few thought Clemson would be . . . in the 24-team field.: "Tigers Come on Strong."

31   "I dreamed about this earlier . . . could win the championship.": "Tigers Come on Strong."

32   As he stepped into the huddle, . . . not about to happen.": Tim Crothers, "Woody to the Rescue," *Sports Illustrated,* Nov. 27, 2000, http://vault.sportsillutrated.cnn.com/vault/article/magazine/MAG1021203/index.htm, Feb. 26, 2009.

32   Asked after the game . . . from watching his father fight.: Crothers.

33   The athletic council met . . . seconded his own nomination.: Sherman, p. 75.

33   He originally received . . . formalized the deal.: Sahadi, p. 51.

33   The president who originally hired . . . didn't get the raise, though.: Sahadi, p. 53.

34   One of the all-time great untold stories." Bob Spear, "From Intramural to Clemson Lore," *The State,* Feb. 2, 2006, http://docs.newsbank.com/s/InfoWeb/aggdocs/NewsBank/10F91A389EF0E9E8, May 5, 2009.

34   With 54 seconds to play, . . . and making those fouls shots.": Spear, "From Intramural."

35   The McSwain brothers were two . . . all the way across the room.": Tysiac, *Tales,* p. 63.

35   "would go out to eat, . . . they decided to room together,: Tysiac, *Tales,* p. 64.

36   the ninth-ranked Seminoles were . . . before they were set.": Ron Morris, "Quick Thinking Saves Clemson," *The State,* Sept. 17, 2006, http://docs.newsbank.com/InfoWeb/aggdocs/NewsBank/1143D81CE78B98A0, May 5, 2009.

37   They cooked up a deal with . . . what the boys want most.": John F. Stegeman, *The Ghosts of Herty Field* (Athens: The University of Georgia Press, 1997), p. 65.

37   Clemson's brilliant left end . . . who was bigger and stronger.: Sahadi, p. 14.

37   they managed to round up . . . ship them to the Clemson players.: Bill Cromartie, *Clean Old-Fashioned Hate* (Huntsville, AL: The Strode Publishers, 1977), p. 34.

38   Terry Don Phillips labeled him . . . McLellan "had great foresight." Tysiac, *Tales,* p. 21.

38   among the first in the country . . . the model for other universities.: Tysiac, *Tales,* p. 21.

38   "He just had great vision,": Tysiac, *Tales,* p. 21.

38   In 1976, he hired the late George Dostal, . . . on stretching and cross training.: Tysiac, Tales, pp. 23-24.

38   One of the Nebraska coaches . . . credit for what happened here.": Tysiac, *Tales,* p. 24.

39   "I'm a Christian and very proud . . . every area as they choose.": "Have Faith; the Recruits Will Come," *The State*, Feb. 5, 2009, http://docs.news-bank.com/s/InfoWeb/aggdocs/NewsBank/12629DA4172F4998, May 13, 2009.

39   Safety Jonathan Meeks said the . . . they get a personal answer.: "Have Faith."

39   To me, religion – faith – is the only real thing in life.: Jim & Julie S. Bettinger, *The Book of Bowden* (Nashville: TowleHouse Publishing, 2001), p. 44.

40   In the first of a three-game set, . . . Matthew LeCroy that tied the game.: Blackman, p. 114.

40   It's amazing. Some of the . . . to be a Christian man.: Bettinger, p. 121.

41   The Tigers stayed at the . . . when they came sneaking in.: Sahadi, p. 179.

41   "Howard gave them a verbal . . . rings in their ears,": Sherman, p. 89.

41   "they were too sorry to play . . . in the morning on the bus.: Sahadi, p. 179.

41   "I got to thinking to myself . . . into this too deep.": Sahadi, p. 179.

41   He decided to let the team . . . make sure they voted "right.": Sherman, p. 89.

42   "There wasn't momentum. . . . winning this game. None.": Paul Strelow, "Tigers Trounce No. 4 Blue Devils," *The State*, Feb. 6, 2009, http://docs.newsbank.com/s/InfoWeb/aggdocs/NewsBank/1262F328EE088008, May 6, 2009.

42   "were ready for this atmosphere. . . . as the game went along.": Strelow, "Tigers Trounce No. 4 Blue Devils."

43   "He's not fat fat. He's just hungry.": Alexander Wolff, "The Paws Have Given Cause for Pause," *Sports Illustrated*, Nov. 16, 1981, http://vault.sports-illustrated.cnn.com/vault/article/magazine/MAG1124980/2/index.htm, Feb. 26, 2009.

43   Perry Tuttle and Jeff Davis were his . . . together like a sandwich.: Tysiac, *Tales*, p. 49.

43   His sophomore season Perry . . . every single one of them.": Tysiac, *Tales*, p. 52.

43   I really ain't much . . . don't mind talking for it.: Bradley, p. 25.

44   Six players from the 1978 team . . . Tuttle and Terry Kinard: Bradley, p. 101.

44   According to Clark, Walsh . . . Clark obliged.: "Dwight Clark," *Wikipedia, the free encyclopedia*, http://en.wikipedia.org/wiki/Dwight_Clark, March 2, 2009.

45   His training methods include Morning Madness, . . . one last time.: Blackman, p. 173.

45   Kriese used a ball of kite string and two upperclassmen as pacers.: Blackman, pp. 173-74.

45   He tied fifteen feet . . . with the string in hand.": Blackman, p. 174.

46   Priester chose Clemson out of . . . in a 13-0 win over Maryland.: Neil White, "Priester Lives How He Runs: Straight Ahead," *The State*, Oct. 12, 2008, http://docs.newsbank.com/s/InfoWeb/aggdocs/NewsBank/123C5FC9382C8DE0, May 6, 2009.

47   The contest in Atlanta was billed . . . against the City Slickers.: Bradley, p. 1.

47   "scrawny, anything-but-tough . . . a big evening of it.":

Sherman, pp. 6-7.

47   Heisman had rounded up . . . Blue Ridge yawns its greatness.'": Sherman, p. 7.

47   When you run trick plays . . . folks question your sanity.: Bettinger, p. 32.

48   They were pranksters. They even . . . drive one another nuts.": Tysiac, *Tales*, p. 58.

48   They took particular delight in . . . had called Berryhill's grandmother.: Tysiac, *Tales*, p. 59.

49   Alan Johnstone was a junior . . . last surviving member of that team: Bob Gillespie, "Clemson Golf Roots Live with 92-Year-Old," *The State*, July 23, 2003, http://docs.newsbank.com/s/InfoWeb/aggdocs/NewsBank/0FC7F3D CF1D63779, May 5, 2009.

49   becoming the first team in NCAA . . . title in the same year.: "2003 National Champions," *Clemson Golf 2008-09*, p. 63, http://grfx.cstv.com/photos/schools/clem/sports/m-golf/auto_pdf/golf_09_mg_055-070.pdf. June 26, 2009.

49   Before the 2003 season began, . . . wanted to have a golf team.": Gillespie, "Clemson Golf Roots."

49   Life is an adventure. . . . going to happen next.: Bettinger, p. 74.

50   Fuller got into the act because . . . never would've lived it down.": Bob Gillespie, "Steve Fuller: Shuffle Lives On," *The State*, Feb. 4, 2007, http://docs.newsbank.com/s/InfoWeb/aggdocs/NewsBank/1172116A332AB1A0, May 6, 2009.

51   the greatest all-round athlete in Clemson history.: "Clemson Legend Banks McFadden Passes at Age 88," *TigerNet*, June 4, 2005. http://www.thetigernet.com/view/story.do, Feb. 23, 2009.

51   the first athlete in collegiate history . . . the same calendar year.: Sherman, p. 65.

51   At a track meet, . . . a foot further from the takeoff board.: Sherman, p. 68.

52   recording what was then a school-record . . . in league history to be so honored.: Will Vandervort, "Former Clemson Star Adds to His Storybook Career," *upstatetoday.com*, May 10, 2007, http://www.upstatetoday.com/news/2007/may/10, March 4, 2009.

52   "It is hard to believe a linebacker can get soft": Vandervort.

52   the announcement in May 2007 . . . be enshrined in the hall.: Vandervort.

53   One of the great college hymns.": Mark Spede, "The Mystery of the Clemson Alma Mater," *Clemson University Tiger Band: History of the Clemson Alma Mater*, http://www.clemson.edu/tigerband/History_AlmaMater.htm, April 16, 2009.

53   In 1918, during the final months . . . used during football games.: Sahadi, p. 19.

53   One student, Albert C. Corcoran, went back . . . "Above Cayuga's Waters.": Sahadi, p. 21.

53   The glee club first performed . . . the one still used today.: Spede.

54   Bob Fulton was the voice . . . I never got one letter of complaint.": "Fulton Remembers '58 Tigers Run," *The State*, May 16, 2008, http://docs.newsbank.com/s/InfoWeb/aggdocs/NewsBank/120B42C489379A98, May 6, 2009.

54   he never left the . . . It worked pretty well.": "Fulton Remembers."

55   Three years into Tuttle's pro . . . to come into my life.": Martin, p. 48.

55   his phone rang. Coach Dan . . . he had been traded.: Martin, p. 48.

55   The Lord allowed my whole . . . to draw me to Him.: Martin, p. 48.

56   White meat.": Bob Gillespie, "All the Talk Aside, Numbers Are 29-0,"
      The State, Sept. 5, 1990, http://docs.newsbank.com/s/InfoWeb/aggdocs/
      NewsBank/0F0F829BE777E016, May 6, 2009.

56   Once as Howard strolled . . . yo' granddaddy said, too.": Gillespie, "All the
      Talk Aside."

56   The rumor mill insisted that . . . and nothing to gain.: Gillespie, "All the
      Talk Aside."

57   With 11:21 remaining, the Terps . . . dismayed and silent Maryland crowd:
      Paul Strelow, "Thriller: Tigers Toast the Terps," *The State*, March 3, 2008,
      http://docs.newsbank.com/s/InfoWeb/aggdocs/NewsBank/0EB585C960B
      33B43, May 6, 2009.

58   "turned Clemson from virtually . . . a southern powerhouse.": "Former
      Head Coaches," *2008 Clemson Football*, p. 170, http://grfx.cstv.com/photos/
      schools/clem/sports/m-footbl/auto_pdf/08_mg_161-176. pdf, June 11, 2009.

58   his players couldn't eat pork . . . hot water in the shower.: Clyde Bolton,
      War Eagle (Huntsville, AL: The Strode Publishers, 1973), p. 68.

58   "should be masterful and . . . little short of a czar.": Bolton, pp. 67-68.

58   On the players' lockers, . . . "don't lose the game.": Bolton, p. 70.

58   No end runs on first or . . . the best down to pass on;: Bolton, p. 69.

58   punts on first down . . . punt anyway, anywhere.": Bolton, p. 70.

59   "the most exciting 25 seconds . . . started out from necessity.: "Clemson
      Tigers: Traditions: The Hill," http://clemsontigers.cstv.com/sports/m-foot-
      bl-the-hill.html, Feb. 25, 2009.

59   The first 20,000 seats in . . . which was operated by hand.": Clemson Tigers:
      Traditions: The Hill."

59   The team members started rubbing . . . the frenzy starts in earnest.:
      "Clemson Tigers: Traditions: The Hill."

60   Clemson had no way to . . . and not get[ting] the kick off.: Bradley, p. 133.

60   We practice running on the field . . . too well last week.": Bradley, pp.
      133-34.

61   "was ahead of its time in almost every respect.": Tysiac, *Tales*, p. 76.

61   After the one-win season . . . will give ten dollars every year.": Sherman,
      p. 71.

61   "born with a silver spoon . . . during its first year.": Sherman, p. 73.

61   "the heart, the life's blood, the muscle of the Clemson athletic program.":
      Sherman, p. 74.

61   "We do not choose whether . . . the foundation on which we will stand.":
      R. Alan Culpepper, "The Gospel of Luke," *The New Interpreter's Bible*, Vol.
      IX (Nashville: Abingdon Press, 1998), p. 153.

62   he had worked on the sidelines . . . respected everywhere in this country,":
      "Fred Hoover: Profile," http://clemsontigers.cstv.com/genrel/hoover_
      fred00.html, June 16, 2009.

62   "one of the most recognized people ever in Clemson athletics." Blackman,
      p. 53.

62   Howard was in Tallahassee . . . the job if he wanted it.": Blackman,
      p. 53.

63   the School of Architecture presented him . . . ever to earn

an architecture degree.: Tim Bourret, "Cliff Hammonds," *Above & Beyond: Clemson 2008-09 Basketball*, p. 91, http://grfx.cstv.com/photos/schools/clem/sports/m-baskbl/auto_pdf/0809mg_080-096.pdf, March 4, 2009.

63 he was totally dehydrated after the game, . . . He came by it naturally.": Bourret.

63 I did such a good job . . . he went to South Carolina.: Bradley, p. 30.

64 When football began at Clemson, . . . picked their own coach,: Bradley, p. 5.

64 chose the school colors of purple and gold and the school mascot.: Sherman, p. 1.

64 The players didn't wear helmets . . . their hair grow long.: Bolton, *War Eagle*, p. 45.

64 A nose guard was about . . . in a hand and pass.: Clyde Bolton, *The Crimson Tide* (Huntsville, AL: The Strode Publishers, 1972), p. 46.

64 A player might hide the ball under his jersey.: Bolton, *War Eagle*, p. 69.

64 Spectators often got in . . . rushing onto the field.: Bolton, *War Eagle*, p. 49.

64 Players dragged tackled ball carriers forward.: Bolton, *War Eagle*, p. 81.

64 Teams decided upon the length . . . they showed up to play.: Bolton, *War Eagle*, p. 80.

64 Linemen held hands and . . . before a play began.: Bolton, *The Crimson Tide*, p. 47.

64 handles were sewn . . . carriers easier to toss.: Bolton, *War Eagle*, p, 81.

64 I'm not to proud . . . to win too much.: Bettinger, p. 15.

65 To be able to say I . . . nobody can take away from me.": Jon Solomon, "Clemson Class Values Perfect Tenure," *The State*, Nov. 15, 2005, http://docs.newsbank.com/s/InfoWeb/aggdocs/NewsBank/10DEBBDB5CA73098, May 5, 2009.

65 Coach Tommy Bowden considered benching . . . said, "Go to work.": Ron Morris, "Clemson Comes Up with the Big Play – As Usual," *The State*, Nov. 20, 2005, http://docs.newsbank.com/s/InfoWeb/aggdocs/NewsBank/10E061D185AF1FB8, May 5, 2009.

66 Don't come home. Find a job." . . . to practice wearing jewelry.: Ken Tysiac, "Herring's Tough Love Unites Tigers Defense," *The State*, Sept. 22, 2000, http://docs.newsbank.com/s/InfoWeb/aggdocs/NewsBank/0EAC559D4B5E9C9A, May 5, 2009.

66 "Our defense reflects Reggie's . . . emotion and great intensity.": Tysiac: "Herring's Tough Love."

67 In November 2007, Kriese . . . would be his last.: Paul Strelow, "Clemson's Kriese Leaves for Thailand," *The State*, May 4, 2008, http://docs.newsbank.com/s/InfoWeb/aggdocs/NewsBank/12074E83533E0680, May 6, 2009.

67 Kriese always insisted that . . . work ethic was superior.": Robert Davis, "Goodbye, Chuck," May 7, 2008, http://clemsontigers.cstv.com/sports/m-tennis/spec-rel/050708aab.html, June 10, 2009.

67 When he announced his resignation, . . . peace in our hearts about going.": Strelow.

68 "one of the most bitter . . . of the Danny Ford era.": Bradley, p. 119.

68 With only 1:18 left on the clock, . . . proper possession of the pass.": Bradley, p. 119.

68 None of us wants justice . . . we'd all go to hell.": Bettinger, p. 69.

69   When the fans saw . . . they roared in approval.: William F. Reed, "The Tigers' New Stripes," *Sports Illustrated*, Nov. 4, 1991, http://vault.sportsillustrated.ccn.com/vault/article/magazine/MAG1140323/index.htm, Feb. 26, 2009.

69   After warming up in their . . . the fans really liked it.": Reed.

70   In 2003, a *Baseball America* . . . $5 million worth of renovations and improvements.: "Doug Kingsmore Stadium," *2009 Clemson Baseball*, p. 116, http://clemsontigers.cstv.com/photos/schools/clem/sports/m-basebl/auto_pdf/09_mg_116-119.pdf, March 3, 2009.

70   In 2000, after Clemson swept . . . we join another conference.": "Doug Kingsmore Stadium," p. 116.

71   You're 5'6" tall. You weigh 152 pounds.: Martin, p. 115.

71   even coaches from smaller colleges . . . any more small, slow football players.": Martin, p. 116.

71   when defensive backs coach Curley . . . what he was capable of.: Martin, p. 117.

71   The next day Martin was in . . . Martin made a solo tackle.: Martin, p. 118.

71   Set your goal to be pleasing to God.: Martin, p. 119.

72   such a Clemson enthusiast that . . . rather than miss it,: Blackman, p. 211.

72   "to upgrade the image of . . . the basis for The Paw: Bradley, p. 37.

72   as Wright Bryan, the university's . . . didn't think much of it.: Bradley, p. 38.

73   before the game the players . . . down the skyrocketing score.: Blackman, p. 4

73   The team manager failed . . . and cleared up the problem.: Blackman, p. 11.

74   On Dec. 4, 1999, in the game . . . basketball was over for me.": Ken Tysiac, "A Lesson in Rebounding," *The State*, Jan. 23, 2000, http://docs.newsbank.com/s/InfoWeb/aggdocs/NewsBank/0EAC555C4512F002, May 5, 2009.

74   "Almost like a second chance,": Tysiac, "A Lesson in Rebounding."

75   He is a member of eleven . . . and the Gator Bowl.: Blackman, p. 238.

75   "three wagon greasings from Mobile." . . . weren't enough kids around.: Sahadi, p. 48.

75   Following Howard's retirement from coaching, . . . or a police department.": Bradley, p. 33.

75   Are you sure there is such a place?: Bradley, p. 33.

76   Before his senior season of 2008 . . . by the line this season.": Will Vandervort, "Coaching Bug Bites Clemson's Hutchinson," *The State*, Oct. 8, 2008, http://docs.newsbank.com/s/InfoWeb/aggdocs/NewsBank/123B0CB8F22520B0, May 6, 2009.

76   With three freshmen linemen starting . . . I'd ever get this chance,": Curt McKeever, "Tiger Lineman Goes from Backup to Coach to Starter," *HuskerExtra.com*, Dec. 27, 2008, http://www.huskerextra.com/articles/2009/01/24/football/doc4955778c2d7de277281697.txt, June 8, 2009.

77   The Tigers belonged to the 20-member . . . against top-seeded Wake Forest.: Blackman, p. 264.

77   Instead, the invitation went to . . . they didn't really care too much,: Blackman, p. 265.

77   Years later, McFadden and teammate . . . and not in New York City.: Blackman, p. 265.

77   Nothing is ever as good as it seems or as bad as it seems.: Martin, p. 120.
78   Ford admitted he "was at . . . changed this team's attitude.": Bradley, p. 152.
78   saying his team had been . . . have fun and just play.": Bradley, p. 153.
79   He prepared for the 1996 season . . . He's gotta have it just perfect,': Josh
      Peter, "The Stuff of Dreams," *The State*, May 14, 1996, http://docs.newsbank.
      com/s/InfoWeb/aggdocs/NewsBank/0EB58568CCDDB88A, May 5, 2009.
80   The Tigers were pounding USC . . . just hovering in mid-air.": Bob
      Gillespie, "Fame First Found Olszewski Long Ago," *The State*, May 4, 1990,
      http://docs.newsbank.com/s/InfoWeb/aggdocs/NewsBank/0F0F8291477
      981E1, May 6, 2009.
81   After high school, Tyner punted . . . to have a solid career.: Ken Tysiac,
      "Diploma 31 Years in the Making," *The State*, Aug. 11, 2002, http://docs.
      newsbank.com/s/InfoWeb/aggdocs/NewsBank/0F55DCA9BAC9E41C,
      May 5, 2009.
81   After a couple of NFL . . . Tyner received his degree.: Tysiac, "Diploma 31
      Years."
82   Asked once if Brett Favre . . . grew up watching Gamecock football.:
      Tysiac, *Tales*, p. 56.
82   His dream was to play . . . seemed like decent guys.": Tysiac, *Tales*, p. 57.
82   the most decorated football player in its history.: Tim Bourret, "Terry
      Kinard: Clemson's Newest Member of the 'Ring of Honor,'" Nov. 5, 2001,
      http://clemsontigers.cstv.com/sports/m-footbl/spec-rel/110501aaj.html, June
      24, 2009.
83   "a quiet, almost subdued . . . never listening to him again.": Josh Peter,
      "Just Call Luckie 'Bo,'" *The State*, Oct. 1, 1996, http://docs.newsback.com/s/
      InfoWeb/aggdocs/NewsBank/0EB585C960B33B43, May 5, 2009.
84   a coal mine,: Blackman, p. 36.
84   a sweat box . . . and a cow palace: Blackman, p. 37.
84   "so-o-o dark that the referees . . . in a small town firehouse.": Blackman,
      p. 37.
85   Ford had his Tigers in Florida early . . . "through a brutal barrage of
      drills.": Tysiac, p. 139.
85   The Tigers ran 40-yard dashes . . . at the point of vomiting.": Tysiac, *Tales*,
      p. 140.
85   Game night in Miami . . . with 74-percent humidity.: Tysiac, *Tales*, p. 139.
85   Nose tackle William Devane looked . . . Jeff Bryant "felt great.": Tysiac,
      Tales, p. 140.
85   "ran out of steam . . . They couldn't do anything.": Tysiac, *Tales*, p. 141.
86   "he had to quit coaching . . . got sick of me.": Bradley, p. 25.
86   his original aim in life . . . be a chicken farmer: Bradley, p. 26.
86   he became a coach because he got to take a shower every day,: Bradley,
      p. 25.
86   "made the decision last April or May to resign,": Bradley, p. 25.
86   "tried to make it look right . . . but it didn't happen that way.": Bradley,
      p. 32.
86   "without rancor, without bitterness.": Bradley, p. 32.
86   How can football become so . . . pick his own time to go?: Bradley, p. 32.
87   When a reported asked him . . . his team was very little.: Kamon Simpson,
      "Tigers Talk of the Town," *The State*, Nov. 23, 1997, http://docs.newsbank.

<table>
<tr><td></td><td>com/s/InfoWeb/aggdocs/NewsBank/0EB586D70D3922D7, May 5, 2009.</td></tr>
<tr><td>87</td><td>"a 27-point barrage . . . flat, broke and busted.": Simpson.</td></tr>
<tr><td>87</td><td>Tailback Raymond Priester, who rushed for . . . 30 minutes until a bowl game.": Simpson.</td></tr>
<tr><td>88</td><td>Bobby Morris, who caught O'Dell both in high school and at Clemson,: Blackman, p. 215.</td></tr>
<tr><td>88</td><td>"like a radio. Plug him in and he comes on.": Blackman, p. 216.</td></tr>
<tr><td>88</td><td>facing only 28 batters . . . hit to the outfield: Blackman, p. 215.</td></tr>
<tr><td>88</td><td>fanning the first five batters . . . fanned four batters in one inning: Blackman, pp. 215-16.</td></tr>
<tr><td>88</td><td>even once being appointed . . . Bob Smith was injured.: Blackman, p. 216.</td></tr>
<tr><td>89</td><td>As a junior in 1968, Waters . . . "You think you can backpedal?": Steve Wiseman, "Waters' Life Full of Twists," The State, June 22, 2008, http://docs.newsbank.com/s/InfoWeb/aggdocs/NewsBank/121774C494F58638, May 6, 2009.</td></tr>
<tr><td>89</td><td>Stunned, Waters managed to . . . until I got to the NFL.": Wiseman.</td></tr>
<tr><td>89</td><td>"We kind of laughed" about Waters playing defense,: Wiseman.</td></tr>
<tr><td>90</td><td>In 1939, Joe Sherman's job . . make the big All-Americas.",: Blackman, p. 247.</td></tr>
</table>

BIBLIOGRAPHY

"2003 National Champions." *Clemson Golf 2008-09.* 62-63. http://grfx.cstv.com/photos/schools/clem/sports/m-golf/auto_pdf/golf_09_mg_055-070.pdf.

"About Clemson: History." http://www.clemson.edu/about/history.

"Barbara Kennedy-Dixon: Profile." http://clemsontigers.cstv.com/sports/w-baskbl/mtt/kennedydixon_barbara00.html.

Bettinger, Jim & Julie S. *The Book of Bowden.* Nashville: TowleHouse Publishing, 2001.

Blackman, Sam, Bob Bradley, and Chuck Kriese. *Clemson: Where the Tigers Play.* Champaign, IL: Sports Publishing L.L.C., 2001.

Bolton, Clyde. *The Crimson Tide.* Huntsville, AL: The Strode Publishers, 1972.

--- *War Eagle: A Story of Auburn Football.* Huntsville, AL: The Strode Publishers, 1973.

Bourret, Tim. "Cliff Hammonds." *Above & Beyond: Clemson 2008-09 Basketball.* 91. http://grfx.cstv.com/photos/schools/clem/sports/m-baskbl/auto_pdf/0809mg_080-096.pdf.

---. "Terry Kinard: Clemson's Newest Member of the 'Ring of Honor.'" 5 Nov. 2001. http://clemsontigers.cstv.com/sports/m-footbl/spec-rel/110501aaj.html.

Bradley, Bob. *Death Valley Days: The Glory of Clemson Football.* Atlanta: Longstreet Press, 1991.

"Clemson Legend Banks McFadden Passes at Age 88." *TigerNet.* 4 June 2005. http://www.thetigernnet.com/view/story.do.

"Clemson Tigers: Facilities: Memorial Stadium." http://clemsontigers.cstv.com/school-bio/facilities-football.html.

"Clemson Tigers: Traditions: National Championship." http://clemsontigers.cstv.com/sports/m-footbl/spec-rel/021809aab.html.

"Clemson Tigers: Traditions: The Hill." http://clemsontigers.cstv.com/

sports/m-footbl/the-hill.html.

Cole, Bob. "Tigers' Hines Trying to Keep Perspective." *The State.* 7 March 1993. http:// docs.newsbank.com/s/InfoWeb/aggdocs/NewsBank/0F0F8233B158D716.

Cromartie, Bill. *Clean Old-Fashioned Hate.* Huntsville, AL: The Strode Publishers, 1977.

Crothers, Tim. "Woody to the Rescue." *Sports Illustrated.* 27 Nov. 2000. http://vault. sportsillustrated.cnn.com/vault/article/magazine/MAG1021203/index.htm.

Culpepper, R. Alan. "The Gospel of Luke: Introduction, Commentary, and Reflections." *The New Interpreter's Bible.* Nashville: Abingdon Press, 1998. Vol. IX. 1-490.

Dahlberg, Bruce T. "Anger." *The Interpreter's Dictionary of the Bible.* Nashville: Abingdon Press, 1962). Vol. 1. 135-37.

Davis, Robert. "Goodbye, Chuck . . . Farewell to a Coaching Legend." 7 May 2008. http://clemsontigers.cstv.com/sports/m-tennis/spec-rel/050708aab.html.

"Doug Kingsmore Stadium: Home of Tiger Baseball." *2009 Clemson Baseball.* 116-19. http://clemsontigers.cstv.com/photos/schools/clem/sports/m-basebl/auto_ pdf/09_mg_116-119.pdf.

"Dwight Clark." *Wikipedia, the free encyclopedia.* http://en.wikipedi.org/wiki/Dwight_ Clark.

"Former Head Coaches." *2008 Clemson Football.* 170. http://grfx.cstv.com/photos/ schools/clem/sports/m-footbl/auto_pdf/08_mg_161-176. pdf.

Fowler, Scott. "Silver a Bitter Prize for Former Tiger." *The State.* 21 Aug. 2008. http:// docs.newsbank.com/s/InfoWeb/aggdocs/NewsBank/122B3B93902218B0.

"Fred Hoover: Profile." http://clemsontigers.cstv.com/genrel/hoover_fred00.html.

"Fulton Remembers '58 Tigers Run." *The State.* 16 May 2008. http://docs.newsbank. com/s/InfoWeb/aggdocs/NewsBank/120B42C489379A98.

Gillespie, Bob. "All the Talk Aside, Numbers Are 29-0." *The State,* 5 Sept. 1990. http:// docs.newsbank.com/s/InfoWeb/aggdocs/NewsBank/0F0F829BE777E016.

---. "Clemson Golf Roots Live with 92-Year-Old." *The State.* 23 July 2003. http://docs. newsbank.com/s/InfoWeb/aggdocs/NewsBank/0FC7F3DCF1D63779.

---. "Country's Top 'D'? Tigers Showed Illini." *The State.* 2 Jan. 1991. http://docs.news-bank.com/s/InfoWeb/aggdocs/NewsBank/0F0F82A521FFF0D7.

---. "Fame First Found Olszewski Long Ago." *The State.* 4 May 1990. http://docs.news-bank.com/s/InfoWeb/aggdocs/NewsBank/0F0F8291477981E1.

---. "Solomon Proves a Wise Decision." *The State.* 11 Oct. 1992. http://docs.newsbank. com/s/InfoWeb/aggdocs/NewsBank/0F0F822A01ABB365.

---. "Steve Fuller: Shuffle Lives On for Fuller." *The State.* 4 Feb. 2007. http://docs.news-bank.com/s/InfoWeb/aggdocs/NewsBank/1172116A332AB1A0.

"Have Fath; The Recruits Will Come." *The State.* 5 Feb. 2009. http://docs.newsbank. com/s/InfoWeb/aggdocs/NewsBank/12629DA4172F4998.

Johnson, Lorie. "Heart Breaker." *Sharing the Victory Magazine.* Nov. 2006. http://www. sharingthevictory.com/vsItemDisplay.1sp&objectID=D3B21789.

Kirk, Steve. "Clemson's Young Proves It Can Be Done." *The State.* 16 Oct. 1998. http:// docs.newsbank.com/s/InfoWeb/aggdocs/NewsBank/0EB5878CBA49B485.

---. "Tigers Go for NIT Glory." *The State.* 25 March 1999. http://docs.newsbank.com/s/ InfoWeb/aggdocs/NewsBank/0EB587E93001957A.

"Kyle Young: Profile." http://clemsontigers.cstv.com/genrel/young_kyle00.html.

Lucey, Trisha. "Perry Tuttle, Clemson Wide Receiver." *Sports Illustrated.* 14 Dec. 1998. http://vault.sportsillustrated.cnn.com/vault/article/magazine/MAG1014771/ index.htm.

MacArthur, John. *Twelve Ordinary Men*. Nashville: W Publishing Group, 2002.

Martin, Dr. Carl F., Jr. *Real Champions: Tigers Touched by God*. Pickens, SC: E.P.I.C. Publishing, 2001.

Mays, Amanda. "Tigers' 'Rock of Ages': Clemson Lays Howard to Rest." *The State*. 29 Jan. 1996. http://docs.newsbank.com/s/InfoWeb/aggdocs/NewsBank/ 0EB58503B585AFBB.

McCallum, Mark R. "Burnham Gets Bounce Back in His Step." *The State*. 31 March 1995.http://docs.newsbank.com/s/InfoWeb/aggdocs/NewsBank/0EB5845AE8 A7B5E5.

McKeever, Curt. "Tiger Lineman Goes from Backup to Coach to Starter." *HuskerExtra.com*. 27 Dec. 2008. http://www.huskerextra.com/articles/2009/01/24/football/ doc49557782d7de277281697.txt.

Morris, Ron. "Clemson Comes Up with the Big Play – as Usual." *The State*. 20 Nov. 2005.http://docs.newsbank.com/s/InfoWeb/aggdocs/NewsBank/10E061D185 AF1FB8.

---. "Quick Thinking Saves Clemson." *The State*. 17 Sept. 2006. http://docs.newsbank. com/InfoWeb/aggdocs/NewsBank/1143D81CE78B98A0.

Patterson, Lezlie. "ACC Tournament Awaits Clemson, Burgos' 'Weird Stuff.'" *The State*. 19 April 1991. http://docs.newsbank.com/s/InfoWeb/aggdocs/News Bank/0F0F83951E95147C.

---. "Earning His Stripes." *The State*. 7 March 1992. http://docs.newsbank.com/s/ InfoWeb/aggdocs/NewsBank/0F0F839C8388EFF5.

Peter, Josh. "Just Call Luckie 'Bo.'" *The State*. 1 Oct. 1996. http://docs.newsback.com/s/ InfoWeb/aggdocs/NewsBank/0EB585C960B33B43.

---. "Simmons Newest Pupil at Tigers' Linebacker U." *The State*. 21 Sept. 1996. http:// docs.newsbank.com/s/infoWeb/aggdocs/NewsBank/0EB585C1F66260D4.

---. "The Stuff of Dreams." *The State*. 14 May 1996. http://docs.newsbank.com/s/ InfoWeb/aggdocs/NewsBank/0EB58568CCDDB88A.

---. "Tears Mix with Chuckles at Services for Howard." *The State*. 29 Jan. 1996. http:// docs.newsbank.com/s/InfoWeb/aggdocs/NewsBank/0EB58503BB886F90.

Reed, William F. "The Tigers' New Stripes." *Sports Illustrated*. 4 Nov. 1991. http://vault. sportsillustrated.ccn.com/vault/article/magazie/MAG1140323/index.htm.

Rice, Justin A. "Spiller Delivers Knockout Blow." *The State*. 2 Nov. 2008. http://docs. newsbank.com/s/InfoWeb/aggdocs/NewsBank/12434A3FE4C4F2D8.

Sahadi, Lou. *The Clemson Tigers: From 1896 to Glory*. New York: William Morrow & Co., Inc., 1983.

"Shawn Crawford." *Wikipedia, the free encyclopedia*. http://en.wikipedia.org.wiki/ Shawn_Crawford.

Sherman, Joe. *Clemson Tigers: A History of Clemson Football 1896-1977*. Columbia, S.C.: The R.L. Bryan Company, 1976.

Simpson, Kamon. "Tigers Talk of the Town: Clemson Regroups at Halftime." *The State*. 23 Nov. 1997. http://docs.newsbank.com/s/InfoWeb/aggdocs/NewsBank/ 0EB586D70D3922D7.

Solomon, Jon. "Clemson Class Values Perfect Tenure." *The State*. 15 Nov. 2005. http:// docs.newsbank.com/s/InfoWeb/aggdocs/NewsBank/10DEBBDB5CA73098.

Spear, Bob. "From Intramural to Clemson Lore." *The State*. 2 Feb. 2006. http://docs. newsbank.com/s/InfoWeb/aggdocs/NewsBank/10F91A389EF0E9E8.

---. "Love Him, Hate Him, But Never Forget Him." *The State*. 27 Jan. 1996. http://docs.newsbank.com/s/InfoWeb/aggdocs/News

Bank/0F0F82EfFA7E5728.

Spede, Mark. "The Mystery of the Clemson Alma Mater." *Clemson University Tiger Band: History of the Clemson Alma Mater*. http://www.clemson.edu/tigerband/History_AlmaMater.htm.

Stegeman, John F. *The Ghosts of Herty Field*. Athens: The University of Georgia Press, 1997.

Strelow, Paul. "Clemson's Kriese Leaves for Thailand." *The State*. 4 May 2008. http://docs.newsbank.com/s/InfoWeb/aggdocs/NewsBank/12074E83533E0680.

---. "Thriller: Tigers Toast the Terps." *The State*. 3 March 2008. http://docs.newsbank.com/s/InfoWeb/aggdocs/NewsBank/0EB585C960B33B43.

---. "Tigers Trounce No. 4 Blue Devils." *The State*. 6 Feb. 2009. http://docs.newsbank.com/s/InfoWeb/aggdocs/NewsBank/1262F328EE088008.

"Tigers Come on Strong Late in the Season." *Clemson Tigers: Men's Soccer: 1987 National Championship*. http://clemsontigers.cstv.com/sports/m-soccer/specrel/060203aab.html.

Tysiac, Ken. "Diploma 31 Years in the Making." *The State*. 11 Aug. 2002. http://docs.newsbank.com/s/InfoWeb/aggdocs/NewsBank/0F55DCA9BAC9E41C.

---. "Herring's Tough Love Unites Tigers Defense." *The State*. 22 Sept. 2000. http://docs.newsbank.com/s/InfoWeb/aggdocs/NewsBank/0EAC559D4B5E9C9A.

---. "A Lesson in Rebounding: Clemson Senior's Resolve Inspires Team After Heart Surgery." *The State*. 23 Jan. 2000. http://docs.newsbank.com/s/InfoWeb/aggdocs/NewsBank/0EAC555C4512F002.

---. *Tales from Clemson's 1981 Championship Season*. Champaign, IL: Sports Publishing L.L.C., 2006.

Vandervort, Will. "Coaching Bug Bites Clemson's Hutchinson." *The State*. 8 Oct. 2008. http://docs.newsbank.com/s/InfoWeb/aggdocs/NewsBank/123B0CB8F22520B0.

---. "Former Clemson Star Adds to His Storybook Career." *upstatetoday.com*. 10 May 2007. http://www.upstatetoday.com/news/2007/may/10.

White, Neil. "Priester Lives How He Runs: Straight Ahead." *The State*. 12 Oct. 2008. http://docs.newsbank.com/s/InfoWeb/aggdocs/NewsBank/123C5FC9382C8DE90.

Wiseman, Steve. "Waters' Life Full of Twists.": *The State*. 22 June 2008. http://docs.newsbank.com/s/InfoWeb/aggdocs/NewsBank/121774C494F58638.

Wolff, Alexander. "The Paws Have Given Cause for Pause." *Sports Illustrated*. 16 Nov. 1981. http://vault.sportsillustrated.cnn.com/vault/article/magazine/MAG1124980/2/index.htm.

TIGERS

INDEX
(LAST NAME, DEVOTION DAY NUMBER)

198